2104
13.48

M000012689

The
HOLY SPIRIT
and
MISSION
DYNAMICS

RECEIVED MAY 2 5 2012

OTHER TITLES IN EMS SERIES

The
HOLY SPIRIT
and
MISSION
DYNAMICS

C. Douglas McConnell
Editor

Evangelical Missiological Society Series #5

P.O. BOX 40129
PASADENA, CALIFORNIA 91114

Copyright 1997 by Evangelical Missiological Society

All Rights Reserved

No part of this publication may be reproduced, stored in a retrieval system, or transmitted in any form or by any means--electronic, mechanical, photocopy, recording, or any other--except for brief quotations embodied in critical articles or printed reviews, without prior permission of the publisher.

EMS Series #5

Published by
William Carey Library
P. O. Box 40129
Pasadena, California 91114
(818) 798-0819

ISBN 0-87808-379-0

Library of Congress Cataloging-in-Publication Data

The Holy Spirit and mission dynamics / C. Douglas McConnell, editor.
    p. cm. -- (Evangelical Missiological Society series ; no. 5)
    Includes bibliographical references.
    ISBN 0-87808-379-0 (alk. paper)
    1. Missions--Theory. 2. Holy Spirit. I. McConnell, C.
Douglas, 1951- . II. Series.
BV2063.H65   1997
266'.001---dc21   97-28933
                           CIP

5   4   3   2   1
00 99 98 97

PRINTED IN THE UNITED STATES OF AMERICA

Contents

PREFACE

C. Douglas McConnell

As I passed by a classroom on the campus of Fuller Seminary in early 1985, I wondered what or who in the world could draw so many students that they would be hanging out of the door. It seemed odd to me that a seminary class, despite the excellent teachers, would have students so interested that they would actually be standing due to lack of seating. My experience was that standing was a method of handling early or late classes, perhaps even a particular lecturer. But this class was definitely unique. So what was it? It was MC510, Signs, Wonders, and Church Growth. C. Peter Wagner and John Wimber had designed a course in which they examined the role of the Holy Spirit in church growth and missions. As popular as it was with the students, it was equally controversial with the faculty. By 1986, the course had stimulated so much heated discussion that it was withdrawn from the course schedule and the proponents were left to find another curricular approach to deal with the subject.

It appears that the controversial nature of this subject has lost little of its steam in ten years. If anything, it has gained both momentum and profile within the missions community. In a crowded room in Orlando last September, delegates to the triennial conference of the Evangelical Fellowship of Mission Agencies, the Evangelical Missiological Society, and the Interdenominational Foreign Missions Association demonstrated the range of interest shown at Fuller. Wagner kicked off the session with his personal pilgrimage of discovery (chapter six of this volume), followed by responses from four missiologists coming from very different backgrounds and perspectives. The discussion which followed reinforced the observation that interest and controversy continue to surround the work of the Holy Spirit and the dynamics which affect missions today.

Unfortunately, over the past decade there have been few forums in which the controversial nature of the subject could be openly discussed. During the 1994 annual EMS conference, the subject surfaced through a paper which challenged the theory and practice of a number of missiologists. Despite the careful work by the scholars in preparing the paper, there was no real dialogue during the meeting. In fact, the controversial aspects were heightened to the point that the third volume of the EMS series was published as a means of raising the issues within the evangelical missiological community.[1] With the publication of this volume, the dialogue reaches a new level. The ten chapters included here represent an attempt to reflect the concerns and the present understanding of evangelical missiologists, at least those who participated in the conference.

The discussion of the issues which emerge in the three sections of this volume are far from over. In fact, it would benefit all of us if we could continue the dialogue in forums and subsequent publications, particularly the issues of advocacy, epistemology, hermeneutics, historiography, philosophy, and theology raised in part three. Perhaps Gary McGee stated it best in the conclusion of his article,

> Today, the increasing interest in strategic-level spiritual warfare has raised major questions about the believer's authority over the powers of darkness. This requires that related exegetical, theological, and missiological issues receive careful and irenic scrutiny by both practitioners and scholars. Their dialogue on ministry in the power of the Spirit offers a unique opportunity for evangelical Chris-

---

[1] Edward Rommen, ed., *Spiritual Power and Missions: Raising the Issues* (Pasadena: William Carey Library, 1995).

tians of all persuasions to grow in mutual understanding, work together for the advancement of the
kingdom of God, and realize greater unity in the
body of Christ.

If the EMS can become such a forum and provide the
opportunity to publish carefully written contributions to the
dialogue, then it will indeed fill a unique need in the missions community.

In any compilation of articles such as this one, the
editor has the daunting task of trying to arrange the individual contributions within the framework of a set topic. In an
effort to impose a standard format, we used both *The Tyn-
dale Manual of Style* (1991) and the *Publication Manual of The
American Psychological Association*, 4th edition, (1994). I
would like to acknowledge the contribution of Gary Corwin
and Jim Reapsome, members of the ad hoc editorial committee, who greatly assisted in the structure and content of this
volume. I was also encouraged in my efforts by Gailyn Van
Rheenen, publications committee chair, and the executive of
the EMS. Finally, the vital contributions of Emily Moreau, as
technical reader, and the administrative assistance of Carol
Fowler and Janna McConnell are greatly appreciated.

AUTHOR PROFILES

Roland Allen (1868-1947), was a British missionary statesman and author. He was an ordained Anglican minister and served as a missionary in China.

Don N. Howell, Jr. is Professor of Bible, Greek, and Theology, and Assistant Dean of the Seminary. He has served as a missionary in Japan.

C. Douglas McConnell is an Associate Professor of Missions & Intercultural Studies and Department Chair at Wheaton College. He served as a missionary in Australia and Papua New Guinea. He is the editor of the *Occasional Bulletin* of the EMS.

Gary B. McGee is a Professor of Church History at the Assemblies of God Theological Seminary. He is an ordained minister and has consulted widely with the Division of Foreign Missions for The General Council of the Assemblies of God.

Robertson McQuilkin is the President Emeritus of Columbia International University. He served as a missionary in Japan and as the Executive Director of the EMS.

A. Scott Moreau is an Associate Professor of Missions and Intercultural Studies at Wheaton College. He served as a missionary in South Africa and Kenya.

John Orme is the Executive Director of the Interdenominational Foreign Mission Association. He served as a missionary in Guatemala.

Michael Pocock is Professor and Chairman of World Missions and Intercultural Studies at Dallas Theological Seminary. He served as a missionary in Venezuela. He is the President of the EMS.

Robert J. Priest is an anthropologist and an Associate Professor of Missions and Intercultural Studies at Columbia International University. He has done field work in South America.

Gailyn Van Rheenen is an Associate Professor of Missions at Abilene Christian University. He served as a missionary in Uganda and Kenya. He is the Chairman of the Publications Committee of the EMS.

C. Peter Wagner is the Donald A. McGavran Professor of Church Growth and Dean of Fuller Colorado at Fuller Theological Seminary. He served as a missionary in Bolivia.

PART I

BIBLICAL THEOLOGICAL ISSUES

Our starting point for the study of the Holy Spirit and mission dynamics is Scripture. A biblical theological perspective provides us with the necessary understandings from which to assess the phenomena we observe in both history and our contemporary mission practice. In this section, Michael Pocock gives an overview of the critical issues facing the missions community. He takes a careful look not only at the dynamics of missions, but also reminds us that missions is a "project authorized by God."

In looking at the role of the Holy Spirit, Robertson McQuilkin examines eight activities of the Spirit with regard to missions. Additionally, Scripture makes it quite clear that the means of connecting with the power of the Holy Spirit is through prayer, which is the conclusion to McQuilkin's contribution. He achieves his goal of providing a good outline of the biblical teaching on the Holy Spirit.

In the third chapter, Don Howell deals with the centrality of the Holy Spirit to the work of the apostle Paul. Beginning with the writings of Roland Allen, Howell treats 1 and 2 Thessalonians in depth, providing a solid treatment of both the text and the implications for missions. It is refreshing to read the work of one so committed to biblical scholarship, yet with a knowledge of mission practice.

Although other contributors deal with biblical theology, this section provides the biblical basis in a way that is more clearly focused on Scripture. While this is a good start, there remains a great deal of work to be done in the intersection of pneumatology and missiology.

7

1

MISSIOLOGY AND SPIRITUAL DYNAMICS: AN OVERVIEW OF THE ISSUES

Michael Pocock

Some years ago I sat on the platform looking out at an excited congregation of about 90 Venezuelans whom the Lord had brought together as a new church. I had known some of them three years before when my wife and I arrived in Valencia. It was a deeply satisfying moment to be present as that congregation was fully constituted as a church with leadership in place and a bright future. A thought came to me: "Who was responsible for all this?"

As I looked at one new believer after the other, I realized that Dona Debora had won Lilita to the Lord. Augusto had attracted and won a number. Romulo had witnessed to Kenneth, and Carlos came to Christ when someone shared a testimony at a beach party. Some had listened to TransWorld Radio. Campus Crusade workers and my own coworkers from TEAM had all helped greatly. Teo—the pastor today—had just dropped in with a friend and responded to the first evangelical message he ever heard.

What came over me was the distinct impression that God had done something around me, above and beyond me, as well as through me. In a sense I had simply been there and God used me to congeal a work of the Spirit in my presence. The Lord of the harvest did the work of ministry—a work to which I bore only incidental relationship. Today that church exists and has grown in spite of many trials— and is pastored by one who found Christ in the earliest days of the church's existence. So it stands confirmed, what Jesus said in Matthew 6:18, "I will build my church and the gates of Hades will not overcome it."

Missionary work depends on spiritual dynamics. When the apostles were filled on the day of Pentecost, that's all they had, a great inner spiritual dynamic who was the Holy Spirit. They didn't have much or any education. They didn't know that people in transition are more open to new ideas. They knew nothing about diffusion of innovation theory.[1] They didn't know that peoples everywhere like to become Christians without crossing barriers of race, language and class.[2] They had no tools like printed material, films and videos or the gospel on recordings they could listen to with hand-cranked audio players—all that was yet to come. They simply had the Holy Spirit, the Word of God, the authenticity of Christ and a practical grasp of the relationship between prayer and fasting and spiritual work.

Across the EMS last year, we studied the relationship of the social sciences to missiology.[3] On reflection, I don't think anyone would want to do without key insights from these sciences that have helped the work of missions. As we have striven to understand cultures, movements of peoples, how cultures decide, to say nothing of technologies that also aid missions—and the collection of data that informs missiology, I believe we were convinced that science and technology play a key role. On the other hand, I believe we saw them as having a *ministerial* rather than *magisterial* relationship to missions. The sciences are *handmaids* of missions, but they do not constitute what causes spiritual change to occur. "The Spirit gives life, the flesh counts for

---

[1] Dayton, Edward, and Fraser, David. *Planning Strategies for World Evangelization.* (Grand Rapids: Eerdmans Publishing Company, 1980), 315-16.

[2] McGavran, Donald. *Understanding Church Growth.* rev. ed. (Grand Rapids: Eerdman's, 1970), 223.

[3] Now available in vol. 4 in the EMS series. This volume edited by Ed Romman is *Missiology and The Social Sciences.* (Pasadena: William Carey Library, 1996).

nothing. The words that I have spoken to you are spirit and they are life" (John 6:63).

As we study the Spiritual Dynamics of Missions this year, we are looking at the fundamental causative factors which bring about spiritual change in the lives of people. Some of these factors will doubtless be:

The Extent to Which Missions
Is a Project Authorized by God

Most of us have this matter settled in our hearts already based on clear passages of Scripture which we can cite from memory. But we should recall that the church has not always been confident of this authority. Some have believed that although Christ clearly commissioned the disciples to do a cross-cultural discipleship task among all nations (Matt 28:18-20), that commission was discharged by the original apostles and no longer applies to Christians in general.

Our certainty about how or if the great commission really applies is also eroded whenever credence is given to the salvific possibilities of spiritual experiences outside of conscious faith in Christ. The Catholics at Vatican II said the people of God were not only those "possessing the Spirit of Christ," but also "those who have not received the gospel . . . those who acknowledge the Creator . . . Moslems . . . (and) those who in shadows and in ages seek the unknown God . . . ."[4]

In some Protestant evangelical circles, salvation and relation to God has been claimed to be possible without ex-

---

[4]"Dogmatic Constitution in the Church," from Vatican II, Lumen Gentium in Flannery, (Austin, O.P. Ed. *Vatican Council II*, rev. ed. 1992), 336-68.

plicit faith in Christ.[5] The imperative nature of a missionary movement has been compromised wherever universalism appears and even where a wider hope is entertained, in spite of John Sanders' claim to the contrary.

Among those who accept the continuing authority to engage in missions, there are still the questions of *how much* Christ authorized the apostles to do and *how much* continues as the responsibility and privilege of believers today. The apostles were told at one point to preach the gospel of the kingdom, heal the sick, cast out demons and raise the dead (Matt 10:1-10). Jesus told the apostles in the great commission passage of Matthew 28:19-20 that they should teach *their* disciples "to observe (or obey) all things that I have commanded you." Does this really mean "everything" —or what might be left out? No doubt we will discuss this at this conference because there are questions among us about whether our power to minister relates to *testifying* about authenticating events and miracles in the past or *demonstrating* God's power in miracles today.

In addition to the confidence God gives to missionaries through the authority granted (so that we don't feel as if we are fishing without a license, even if some of the streams are posted by the inhabitants!), God has made certain promises about the dynamic factors which make the missionary enterprise possible: the promise that the Holy Spirit would energize missionary work (Acts 1:8); that when the Holy Spirit was given, he would perform certain works *on* the unregenerate and *in* the Christian minister; he would convict of sin (Jn 16:7-11); he would bring back to the mind of the minister the teaching of Christ (Jn 14:25-26); he would reside in the very words of truth given by Christ which would have the power to free people from bonds of sin and enslavement to Satan (Jn 8:31-32; Jn 17:13-19); and the

---

[5]Sanders, John, *No Other Name* (Grand Rapids: Eerdmans, 1992) 263-67.

promise of Christ's presence with the evangelist at all times (Mt 28:20). The understanding that we are involved in a fully authorized enterprise is a central spiritual dynamic that gives confidence, boldness and a sense of legitimate freedom in missions today. We are not "fishing without a license"!

The Dynamic of Strength Through Relationship With Others in the Task

It is interesting that when Jesus first chose the disciples, the reason cited was "to be with him, and that he might send them forth to preach . . ." (Mk 3:14). Jesus did his own work in relation to other people. He is hardly ever found ministering alone. Men, and women, constantly accompanied Jesus in his work (Lk 8:1-3) and when he sent out two "pilot projects," the workers were sent in pairs (Lk 10:6).

Paul seems to pick up on this idea (yet it may have come directly from the Spirit of God) when he and Barnabas were sent out from Antioch (Acts 13:1-4). Paul's missionary band grew to where ten others are mentioned as accompanying him (Acts 20:1-4). He frequently expresses thanks for coworkers—again both men and women—indicating the degree to which their companionship and fellowship in the work helped to energize him. At one point Paul indicates that he "had no peace" when he was in Troas, waiting for others to join him (2 Cor 2:13). We need to further explore the point that relationship to others in ministry is not simply a nice option but a basic dynamic in missions work.

The Dynamics of Spiritual Disciplines

Jesus modeled the indispensability of prayer and urged his followers to "pray to the Lord of the harvest to send out workers into his harvest field . . ." (Matt 9:38). The first sending of workers by a church in Acts 13:1-4 shows that the awareness of who should be sent came in the context of worship—doubtless prayer, too—and fasting. Studies have been made that directly link prayer to effectiveness in ministry.[6] Without considering it to be a magical formula, studies have shown that the amount of prayer makes a difference in missionary work. On average, church planters with effective, growing churches spent four and a half hours more a week than less "successful" church planters.

The apostle Paul asked for prayer relative to new preaching opportunities, for courage in preaching, and for clarity and expression (Eph 6:19-20). He also asked for prayer for protection from unbelievers (Rom 15:31). One of the great benefits of the recent "Light The Window" campaign has been to focus specific prayer for cities in the 10-40 window[7] and, of course, Patrick Johnstone has long provided the data and encouragement for prayer through Operation World.[8] Others will develop this dynamic further so I will desist in this presentation.

---

[6]Grady, Dick and Kendall, Glenn, "Seven Keys to Effective Church Planting," *Evangelical Missions Quarterly*, (Wheaton: Evangelical Missions Information Service, 1992), 28:366-73, cited in Ray Gorrell, "Overcoming Obstacles To Church Planting in S.E. France" (Unpublished D. Min. dissertation, Dallas Theological Seminary, 1996).

[7]Wagner, C. Peter, Peters, Stephen, and Wilson, Mark, eds. *100 Gateway Cities of the 10-40 Window.* (Seattle: YWAM Publishing, 1995).

[8]Johnstone, Patrick. *Operation World*, Fifth Edition. (Grand Rapids: Zondervan, 1993).

The Dynamics of the Word of God

We need to consider the question of how essential it is to use the written Word of God, not only to set the parameters of what we do and what we understand about the Lord, but in the *doing* of ministry. We are familiar with passages of Scripture that describe the Word of God as a living sword with powerful inherent capabilities (Eph 6 and Heb 4:12). We have already alluded to the truth of the Word that sets men free (Jn 8:31-32). We should also look at the truth that Jesus is the living *Logos* (Jn 1:14). So when we use his Word and proclaim or present his person, we are dealing with a powerful dynamic for spiritual change.

Evangelicals have long deemed the written Word of God to be the sole basis for belief leading to salvation and authority in practice, but do they understand it as having power in itself? Some might (and have) criticized what they regard as a magical or animistic use of the Word when it is used in a formulaic manner.[9]

A major factor in current interest in "spiritual mapping" is the ability to understand the situation or the controlling spirits that oppose the gospel through a *rhema* word of God—i.e. a spoken word of God to and/or through a believer in contrast, but not at variance with, the written *logos* word of God. Peter Wagner, drawing strongly from Jack Deere, has presented and developed this idea.[10] As Peter Wagner is presenting at this conference I am sure we will hear more of this matter and have the opportunity to inter-

---

[9]Pyne, Robert and Moore, David. "Neil Anderson's Approach to the Spiritual Life" *Bibliotheca Sacra* 153 (Jan-March, 1996): 86.

[10]Wagner, Peter, *Confronting the Powers*, 52ff cited in Jack Deere, *Surprised by the Power of the Spirit* (Grand Rapids: Zondervan, 1993).

act with him about it. Personally, though I believe in promptings by the Spirit of God, perceptions or discernment about what should be done or said in a particular situation, I am not at ease with Deere's, Wagner's, or Kraft's understanding of *rhema* words of God. This is partly due to: 1. a deep sense of *"sola scriptura"* which includes, I believe, the idea of the perspicacity of Scripture—the fact that Scripture is both clear and sufficient for all spiritual matters; 2. personal experiences where reported predictive words from God never eventuated; and 3. The claim of Scripture itself to be sufficient (II Tim 3:16-17).

I believe that the announcement of a perception that a believer has relative to a "word of faith" or "word of knowledge" elevates that perception to near noncontradictory status. Whereas a more tentative (dare I say, humble?) expression is helpful, but more open, to qualifying ideas from other believers. I do believe that individuals may get clear perceptions of reality from God, which in some cases are a matter of Holy Spirit illumination of Scripture— or even the impressions of Scripture itself in words or ideas that are relevant to a particular occasion. Discernment or wisdom (James 1:4) is also clearly promised and given in Scripture and current experience. The words of wisdom and knowledge referred to in I Corinthians 12:8 may really be such insights, but when given they should be considered for an answering 'amen' on the part of other believers and rigorous comparison with the written Word of God (as the Bereans did when they heard Paul (Acts 17:11), and the Corinthians (1 Cor 14:29).

The question of epistemology and hermeneutics related to what we can discern from God is an important part of Peter Wagner's recent book, *Confronting the Powers*, which was written as a larger response to the article by Priest, Mullen, and Campbell presented at the EMS national conference in 1994 and published in EMS volume III, *Spiritual*

Power and Missions.[11] Since Peter is present at this conference and speaking on related issues, I will leave further elucidation to him and to our membership.

The Dynamics of the Opposition

It is altogether fitting that this conference should discuss what spiritual powers may be holding up the progress of world evangelization, and the manner of dealing with them. Lately, there has been much discussed and written on this issue—motivated, I am sure, by the desire to complete what is so obviously a commission given by God. There is no doubt that he will be glorified by the gathering of a people from all nations following the preaching of his glorious gospel to them. The lateness of the hour as we approach the third millenium is also a motivating factor and the yearning of thousands to see Christ face to face. But what exactly is it that holds up the progress of world evangelization?

Most of us are familiar with II Corinthians 4:4 indicating that the god of this age blinds the eyes of those who do not believe so that they will not believe the glorious gospel of our Lord Jesus Christ. We take this to be Satan and indeed Paul says elsewhere (Eph 6:10-18) that in the Christian life and ministry, we wrestle with spiritual powers, not simply "flesh and blood"—or in other words, resistant people. The question is, in what ways or by what arrangement do Satan and his demons oppose the spread of the gospel, and *has* the gospel, due to their opposition, been delayed in its advance?

Others have taken up, and some at this conference will take up this issue. There *is* biblical evidence that messages of God have been delayed, apparently by opposition from evil spirit beings (Dan 10). We see individuals who are

---

[11]Pasadena: William Carey, 1995.

apparently energized by satanic beings actively opposing gospel presentations as in the case of Elymas in Acts 13:6-12. However, God's angelic messenger *does* get through in Daniel, and the opposition of Elymas, a "child of the devil," does not stop the conversion of the proconsul who is impressed both by what he sees Paul do *and* his teaching about the Lord.

One definitely gets the impression that God is victorious in Christ over Satan in terms of gospel outreach in the New Testament. We do not, however, see much explanation of *how* demonic hierarchies are arranged, territorially or otherwise, and no pattern for dealing with territorial demonic opposition. It is as if the apostles, in full knowledge of the existence of Satan and demons which they acknowledge, choose not to dignify them as having any "right" or "authority"—as being relatively non-consequential—unless they openly present themselves in an opposing mode. In that case they are dealt with. If one were to characterize the overall attitude to Satan and demons in both Old and New Testaments, it would be one of disparagement and minimization in the light of God's almighty power and authority to rule. They are defeated beings. The gospel is the Good News that they are defeated in Christ (I Jn 3:8). Ministry is one of release from the binding and controlling *impression* that people have, that they are either slaves to Satan and demonic idol gods, or to their own sinfulness. Even in the case of believers under severe demonic pressure, influence, or control, the answer is the truth of who's in control (II Tim 2:24-26). To me this is the essence of what I admit to be the struggle of spiritual warfare.

But Satan is not the only opposing force to the spread of the gospel. The world as a system (the pressure of the "group think" of unregenerate humanity) is not a "friend to grace to help me on to God."[12] But how does the world

---

[12]Isaac Watts, "Am I a Soldier of the Cross?" (hymn).

system express itself? More work should be done here, though Bunyan did a great job of it in his classic allegory, *Pilgrim's Progress.* The wonderful thing about Bunyan's work and perspective, however, is that the very title of his work is so positive. It's not entitled *Pilgrim's Potholes*, but *Pilgrim's Progress.* He does take on the sinister side of the world and Satan in his lesser-known work, *The Holy War.*

It is safe to say that Satan "institutionalizes" himself in the world system, so that when we experience difficulties from the world, it is also really from Satan. Satan is "the god of this age" (2 Cor 4:4). The world does oppose the believer and give him many trials, yet—once again—no threat is final, no defeat is inevitable because as Jesus says, "I have overcome the world" (Jn 16:33). The fact and realization of this at a deep existential level is what helps energize believers in tough situations today.

Both non-Christians and believers themselves can be barriers to the program of the gospel because of the flesh. This flesh is an enemy of the Spirit of God (Rom 8:7) and all he wishes to do, yet even here, the victor is Jesus Christ (Rom 7:24-25).

I teach a course on spiritual warfare at Dallas Theological Seminary. I have faced demonized people, most of whom I have understood to be believers, though severely influenced or controlled by demonic beings and by wrong ideas about biblical realities. I have used biblical counseling, sometimes also rebuking opposing spirits. These people have been freed up from bondage. I encourage counselees to be involved, and to take responsibility for their own sin or incorrect grasp of truth through confession and renunciation of them. The flesh is capable of awful things, including occult practices like witchcraft, which is often thought to be purely demonic. Lists are given in Galatians 5:19-21 and Colossians 3:5-9. Some of these, like prolonged anger, are also said to give a place to the devil (Eph 4:26-27). Any of these manifestations of the flesh is very serious and, demons aside, opposes what the Spirit of God is doing in evangelism and sanctification.

In summary, three dynamics are at work in opposition to missionary work: Satan, the world system, and people operating in the flesh. But God, the Lord of the harvest in terms of work, results, and timing, is greater than every opposition that can be imagined. He it is who gives the resources or dynamics for advance in missions, having:

Authorized the venture,
Given patterns of effective ministry,
Provided spiritual power and disciplines, and
Given the liberating word.

In the current dialogue about spiritual dynamics and missiology, we should be encouraged by the extent to which spiritual factors have become so prominent in a task which is so clearly dependent on the supernatural power of God. Yet in every era there is a reflection of the spirit of the age in the life of the church. We should be willing to recognize this historic fact.

Plato, though not a Christian (having been born around 425 B.C.), dominated the thought of the medieval Western church. Aristotle and, as Luther called him, "his wretched moorish interpreter Averoes," dominated the thinking process of Aquinas and broadly beyond from the thirteenth century, really up to the present time. In the shift from supernatural to natural concerns in philosophy, Descartes and Spinoza demonstrated a replacement of faith with reason as a primary epistemalogical tool and the trend continued with John Locke and David Hume in England. Christian thinkers in every century have been influenced by philosophical trends of the day. When it seemed that religious or metaphysical knowledge was not possible through the rational process alone, Kierkegaard proposed the leap of faith to a knowledge of God not tethered to data but understood through the actions of man as a free agent. His ideas were picked up by both the religiously oriented and the non-religiously oriented. As a result, men like Karl Barth and Albert Camus—both existentialists—arrived at opposite polarities, one theistic and the other atheistic.

We have in our lifetimes emerged from what has been called modernism, the acme of human empiricism, and have entered into post-modernism, in which empiricism and materialism are being discarded. Now we have an openness to intuitive subjectivism as far as epistemology is concerned, and since both Western Christianity and philosophy have, in the minds of many, failed to produce solutions to man's dilemma, a pluralistic scouring of all spiritualities is well underway in what we have come to call the New Age movement.

What we must come to terms with in our discussions of spiritual dynamics is that we are as capable of poisoning ourselves with New Age philosophy as we were with secular humanism. The fact that one produced spiritual bankruptcy does not mean we shall be helped in the end by emerging epistemalogical trends on which we attempt to build new understandings of Christian spirituality. We here today are as susceptible to syncretism as any Indian in Chichicastenango, Guatemala, or African in the Cherubim and Seraphim Church of West Africa. May God help us in a swirling world of subjectivity to anchor ourselves afresh in the eternal Word of God in the canonical books of the Old and New Testaments.

2

THE ROLE OF THE HOLY SPIRIT IN MISSIONS

Robertson McQuilkin

Those who planned the program for this annual meeting of the Evangelical Missiological Society felt we should not only address issues involved in the controversies swirling about spiritual power encounter, but that we should pause and reflect on the overall biblical teaching about the Holy Spirit's role in missions and our role in connecting with his power. Surely this should be the focus of our attention as the key issue in missiology today.

My aim has been so to present the work of the Spirit that not only could my statements be proved from Scripture but that the biblical emphases would come out intact as well. I wanted the knowledgeable to say, *Oh, yes, that resonates with Scripture. That sounds like the Bible!* In this essay I'll not try to give a thorough analysis, but rather an outline of Bible teaching and a call back to the fundamentals.

You expect me to say that the Holy Spirit is indispensable to the missionary enterprise. But is he? What would we shut down if the Holy Spirit departed? Harvard University, named in honor of its founder, the Reverend John Harvard, hasn't shut down. It has a nine-billion-dollar endowment, in fact! And with it they accomplish startling advances on many fronts. But to accomplish God's ends in this world requires the supernatural and that means Holy Spirit power. For that he is indeed indispensable. Especially for the cause of world evangelization.

On this we are agreed, at least in theory. But how he goes about his work and how we relate to him are probably the most disputed issues in contemporary missions. The conflict that has hotly engaged our members in regional EMS meetings across the land this year will no doubt continue beyond the annual conference because "power encounter" is a central issue and positions are held with emotional intensity. I am not competent to shed light that might resolve the issues, but I have a great concern to focus our attention, if ever so briefly, on the fundamentals, the biblical emphases on which we must be in agreement. I'm convinced that only with these simple truths will we truly advance the cause of world evangelization.

Let's look first at the eight indispensable activities of the Spirit in missions and then look carefully at the way we can link up with Holy Spirit power.

Eight Activities of the Holy Spirit in Missions

I want to outline the basic biblical teaching on the Spirit's role in missions and illustrate each with a contemporary issue in missiology. I won't try to solve those issues but simply introduce them to illustrate the significance of each activity of the Spirit. If I left out the illustrations, we could easily assent to the theological statement and never face the implications for what we are thinking, saying, and doing in missions.

1. The Holy Spirit Gave the Message

All Scripture is inspired by God and is useful for teaching the truth, rebuking error, correcting faults, and giving instruction for right living (I Tim 3:16 TEV).

Isn't the Book marvelous! What we are to believe and not to believe, Paul says, how we are not to behave and how we are to behave—that covers just about everything.

1) The Spirit through his Word teaches the truth. For example, he teaches through the Word that Jesus alone is savior from hell. Jesus alone? Hell? Today we doubt and debate in so-called evangelical missiological circles such truths revealed by the Spirit, truths that are fundamental to the missionary enterprise. Scripture teaches truth.

2) The Spirit through his Word rebukes error, Paul says. The error, for example, that there are other ways to salvation and other not-so-bad destinations for those who haven't heard of our Savior. If there are other ways and other destinies, why are we in the missionary business at all? Scripture rebukes the error of neo-universalism, the "wider hope," and annihilationism, positions gaining adherents rapidly in evangelical circles.

3) The Spirit through his Word corrects faults. The fault, for example, of a missionary dominating the young church he comes to serve, or using the gospel message to make gain, psychological if not financial.

4) The Spirit through his Word gives instruction for right living. Love, for example, so pervasive, so visible that people will know whose disciples we are. Even among missiologists who differ widely on the role of the Holy Spirit!

The Holy Spirit gave the message—that's his first activity to empower mission.

2. The Holy Spirit Created the Method: the Church

Christ said, "I will build my church" (Matt 16:18), and the book of Acts is devoted to describing how he did it—the Holy Spirit empowering men to start local congregations. Jesus said this church would be invincible—the powers of hell can't overcome it, or even withstand its onslaught. Through much of the 20th century, mission agencies and theological schools emphasized church, the universal church of which they, too, are integral parts. But they downplayed church, the local congregation which is, in fact, what the

Holy Spirit set about building. That seems to be changing now, but more by force than by choice—many churches are demanding full participation in the mission. That is, when they don't supplant the agency and the school altogether! What is the Spirit saying to us about the method he created and owns, the church?

When he gives gifts to his church, the Spirit distributes them among the individual members. That's so no one member will have all the wisdom or power. Let's not try to consolidate the wisdom and authority into the hands of an elite and short-circuit the intentions of the Holy Spirit.

If the method, the church, is truly the idea of the Spirit, what will it look like when he's completed it? We debate that issue, defining and redefining our goal. Is it to start a witnessing church movement in every people group? At least in every group with more than 10,000 people in it? Or is it to disciple every people group? Or perhaps it is to communicate the gospel to every person? Let us constantly remind one another that, since the church is the Spirit's method and he didn't choose to define the end goal very precisely, we must not be too arrogant in our definitions, nor about our strategies built on those definitions. We must let the indispensable Holy Spirit do his thing, seeking ways to best participate with him.

3. The Holy Spirit is the Guide for the Missionary Enterprise

Throughout the book of Acts it was the Spirit who took the initiative. For example, it was in a prayer meeting that he called the senior pastor and his associate in the church at Antioch and started the intentional worldwide missionary outreach of the church (Acts 13:3-4). When Paul and his missionary team miscued on God's strategy, it was the Holy Spirit who stopped them dead in their tracks and redirected them, not once, but twice (Acts 16:6-10) .

The Spirit is the grand strategist. Using the best of biblical, scientific, and practical wisdom in developing our plans, it is still the Holy Spirit who is the grand strategist. Wise the mission leadership that awaits his leadership and is modest about their discernment of it. Our time and place and method may not be his.

4. The Holy Spirit Calls the Messenger

Isaiah (chapter 6) and Paul (Acts 9) had special calls to missionary service. Not all may have such dramatic encounters with God, but it is still the Holy Spirit who chooses, calls, and empowers for missionary vocation. That's what happened in a very undramatic prayer meeting in Antioch (Acts 13) when the Holy Spirit designated the first missionary team. Jerusalem first heard the call, but the church at Jerusalem stayed home. The church at Antioch, though, that's a different story. They were close enough to the Spirit, listening carefully, so that when he called, they were prepared to answer. So today. He is calling, but are we listening? Adding together all the pioneer missionary church starters from west and east, north and south, we are far too shorthanded to get the task accomplished, however "the task" is defined. Someone isn't listening! There are far too many "Jerusalem" churches, stuck at the home base, hassling over their own needs, unwilling to move out until God blasts them out with adversity.

I believe recruiting the task force needed is the most daunting task facing the churches today. We must find the key to unlock the heart of the buster or X-er. That key is held by the Holy Spirit—he's the one who calls. And without that conviction of call we won't take up the difficult task or won't keep at it very long.

5. The Holy Spirit Energizes the Messenger

He alone can empower for supernatural living and supernatural ministry. We call his work the fruit of the Spirit (Gal 5:22-23) and gifts of the Spirit (Rom 12, I Cor 12-14, Eph 4).

1) The fruit. The Spirit is the only one able to work unity among strong-minded pioneers, among people of diverse cultures, among self-oriented, fallen humans. He is the only one who can take a person bent on saving his life and make him willing to throw it away for the sake of the gospel. And to keep on doing it with tough endurance. Those are the evidences of the Spirit at work.

2) The gifts. The Spirit alone can empower for missionary vocation. If a person doesn't have the supernatural gift of evangelism, how can he even begin to do the apostolic thing, planting the church of Christ in places it is not?

The Holy Spirit is indispensable for life and service—he it is who energizes the messenger.

6. The Holy Spirit Confirms That the Message is His by Miracle Signs That Follow (Mark 16:20)

We find it much easier to go to a consistent extreme than to stay at the center of biblical tension. We pronounce the age of miracles past—a self-fulfilling judgment—or we become obsessed with "power encounter." We live in a demon-free world of purely natural phenomena or we demonize everything. Of course, only our opponents would put any of us at either extreme—we would each, no doubt, claim some point of middle ground. And our personal experience surely filters our theological perspective. So let me tell you mine.

Here are some signs that followed and didn't follow my preaching. In direct answer to prayer God touched and healed me of an illness the doctors said was incurable, releasing me for missionary service in Japan. When I arrived there I was greeted with the magnetic pull of Toyama—the city where dozens of missionaries from all over the country and from many mission agencies had gathered. These were the most gifted and godly among us. They fully expected not only healing, but raising the dead. They anticipated the conversion, not merely of millions, but of the entire nation. Should I participate? They said the train was pulling out of the station and I'd better get on board or I'd be left behind. I was left behind. Only to witness the miracle of scores of hopeless men and women transformed into children of God. And Toyama? Within a few years disillusionment set in, the gathered missionaries dispersed, most to leave Japan, some to leave the ministry and one, at least, to leave the faith. And yet, and yet...When it came time to make the most difficult decision of my life—to leave Japan for ministry in America—the Lord vouchsafed to me a remarkable dream. Two, in fact—something I have never experienced before or since but which was much valued by my Japanese friends. It paved the way for them to participate wholeheartedly in my decision to leave them. The Holy Spirit confirms by signs that follow.

No doubt our understanding of the promised "signs that follow" is colored by our personal experience, as mine has been. But that the touch of the supernatural is an essential evidence of the Holy Spirit at work must be granted by all. Given the record of the early church and the instruction of the epistles, it would seem the burden of proof rests on those among us who would restrict the supernatural work of the Spirit to his most important work in missions—regeneration.

A chief battleground in the present controversy about how Holy Spirit power and unholy spirit power encounter one another seems to be Daniel (chapters 9,10,11). It has become the centerpiece of a whole strategy of power encounter which focuses on confronting territorial spirits. In response, several have denied that Daniel's experience speaks at all of a supra-terrestrial cosmic spiritual warfare among good and evil spirits. Maybe the Holy Spirit didn't make the passage clear in answering the questions we put to it so that we would not try to reduce the mysterious powers of the spiritual realm to a formula. In any event, we must not allow the reality of the Spirit's intention to intervene supernaturally in human affairs to be lost in battles over problematic interpretations.

7. The Holy Spirit Convicts of Sin

In fact, that's what he's here for! Christ sent the Spirit expressly to "convict the world of guilt in regard to sin and righteousness and judgment" (John 16.8). If he doesn't do that we can strategize, psychologize, and propagandize till retirement and nothing will come of it.

This work of the Spirit is directly tied in with his original work of creation—creating humankind in the image of God. By making us God-compatible, the Spirit gave us the capacity to belong to God in an intimate love relationship. But by violating that relationship we have been alienated and the image made dysfunctional. Yet it is that basic compatibility, implanted from the start by the Spirit, that makes possible his communication with us, convicting of sin and need.

8. The Holy Spirit Regenerates

This is the critical work of the Spirit in the entire missionary enterprise. This is what all the other activities of the Spirit aim toward and then, in turn, flow from. Until he transforms individuals in their core nature, none of the other activities of the Spirit have meaning (John 3:5-8; Titus 3:5).

But how can we tell when it happens? Are we supposed to? Over the answer to this question the missiological community splits. Are we to avoid the issue, claiming ignorance of that which is the province of God alone to judge, or are we to be fruit inspectors? It is not a merely academic question. It defines our mission. If we are to view all who bear the name "Christian" as out of bounds for evangelism, the face of the whole world changes. Much of South America and Europe, including the northern tier of the CIS, for example, drop off the missionary map.

The January, 1996 issue of the *International Bulletin of Missionary Research* is devoted to the question of proselytizing. The consensus seems to be that "evangelism" is illegitimate, that it is unbiblical proselytization when aimed at members of any church that calls itself Christian. In fact, there are clear indications that we may soon find ourselves in the position of declaring adherents of other *religions* off bounds for evangelism. For many churchmen, Jewish people are already in that category. Strong words are used in the January issue of IBMR to condemn those who evangelize among Orthodox or Roman Catholic adherents.

My conclusion is that only God is the final judge of who has been regenerated, but that he has called us to be interim fruit inspectors. We are not only permitted to evaluate the spiritual need of people, we are required to do so, and we have the Holy Spirit to give us discernment and the holy Book he gave to be the basis for that evaluation. On the other hand, we are not called to render a final judgment, and the part of wisdom may well be to accept a person's claim at face value and then seek to lead them godward from whatever point the Spirit knows them actually to be. If we are successful in this, the Holy Spirit alone may know precisely when he worked the miracle of regeneration.

The eight activities of the indispensable Holy Spirit in missions: the message, his book; the method, his church; the strategy, his initiative; the call of the messenger; the empowerment of the messenger; confirming the message with miracle power; convicting of sin; and regenerating the sinner. The problem is that we tend to catch a vision of one of these activities of the Spirit or a select few and emphasize them all out of proportion to the others. And in this way we distort the vision we do have. But when we see the grand panoply of all the Spirit is about, the thrill of this mighty provision for our missionary enterprise will guide and energize us in the conquest of the nations for King Jesus.

The resources of the infinite God are available. But how do we connect? How does the power flow?

Connecting With Holy Spirit Power

The power connect is an attitude: yield and trust,
The power flow is an activity: prayer.

Until we have an obedient and believing mindset or heart orientation, the deal is off. The Holy Spirit doesn't force his way on us. But if we meet that simple condition— the same faith response that connected us to him in the first place—we are poised to let the power flow. His mighty activity is ready to be unleashed. And we do that through prayer. Prayer is the human conduit of divine energy. As E.M. Bounds said, "Much prayer, much power, little prayer, little power, no prayer, no power." Paul gives straightforward instruction on spiritual warfare in prayer in his letter to the Colossians 4:2-9.

I think we can discern here an outline first of how we are to pray for missions and then of what we are to pray.

1. How to Pray for Missions

Continue earnestly in prayer, being vigilant in it with thanksgiving; meanwhile praying also for us, that God would open to us a door for the word, to speak the mystery of Christ, for which I am also in chains, that I may make it manifest, as I ought to speak (Col 4:2-4,NKJV).

This is a description of spiritual warfare, not a sleepy routine of saying prayers. We are commanded to continue, which implies regular and persistent. The prayer is to be earnest—spiritual warfare, in fact. There's a commentary on this earlier in the second chapter:

> I want you to know how much I am struggling for you and for those at Laodicea, and for all who have not met me personally (Col 2:1, NKJV).

Paul describes a spiritual battle he wages for people he doesn't even know. In fact, he next uses a military term: be vigilant. Not just daily, persistent, earnest prayer but staying on battle alert to pray in between times, sensitive to the Spirit's intimations of special need. Even among people we've never met.

Paul gives one further characteristic of this kind of combat prayer: it's with thanksgiving. I don't think he's saying not to forget to say thankyou when God answers, important as that is, but rather "prayer with thanksgiving," thanking God for the answer even as we ask. In other words, faith-filled prayer. That's the powerful kind. In fact, that's the only kind that prevails in heaven.

The form of the command in both Colossians and Ephesians is plural—"you all pray." This doesn't prove that prayer must be corporate, of course, but the pattern in the early churches was indeed to seek God in corporate prayer, whether on the day of Pentecost, the solving of problems, or the launching of the missionary enterprise. And Christ himself gave a special promise for united prayer (Matt 18:18-20). Indeed, God moves in answer to the united prayer of a believing people. The church at prayer is the secret to success in missions.

But this passage not only tells us how to pray; it also gives an outline of what to pray.

Paul indicates two varieties of prayer. First, as we have seen, he speaks of prayer as a way of life, general prayer combat. Then he says that we should pray also in particular for him and his missionary team. You might call it strategic prayer for the whole cause and tactical prayer for the specific needs and opportunities of particular people.

2. What to Pray for Missions: Strategic Prayer War

1) He names one such prayer—that a door might be opened. For Paul there were far more closed doors than for us. He just didn't acknowledge them! Most of the 10/40 windows are closed, but by concerted prayer by God's people, the united prayer of faith, we believe they will open, just as we watched in astonishment as the iron curtain shattered under prayer assault from Brother Andrew and others who sensed that God's time had come. A prayer barrage was laid against that citadel of the enemy for seven years till the unthinkable happened and entrenched state communism crumbled. So today, the prayer movement has rightly focused on closed doors. But there are other strategic prayers in Scripture.

2) The nations. The Father made a solemn promise to the Son: "Ask of me and I will give you the nations for your inheritance, the uttermost part of the earth for your possession" (Psalm 2:8). The contemporary prayer movement rightly joins the Son in asking the Father for specific nations or ethnic groups that have not yet been given to the Son. Strategic prayer warfare.

3) Harvesters. Another prayer objective was commanded by the Lord himself: "Pray the Lord of the harvest to thrust out laborers into the harvest" (Matt 9:38). The unreaped harvest is greater than it ever was—more lost people now live than all the lost of recorded history who have lived

and died. The laborers are more than ever before but still far too few. Jesus himself gave us the secret to mobilizing the last great assault on the Enemy strongholds: prayer. "Pray and keep on praying," is the force of the verb. Until the Holy Spirit of God thrusts out the laborers. He uses the same verb that is always used when Jesus cast out demons. No gentle invitation, no options for the ones commanded. The strong word is used because not many will do great and difficult things—and keep at it—without some mighty inner compulsion. That's why we must concentrate on this strategic prayer until the Holy Spirit of God thrusts out those pioneer cross-cultural harvesters in sufficient numbers to finish the task.

3. What to Pray for Missionaries: Tactical Prayer War

Paul gives two specific prayer requests when he asks them to pray for his missionary team and notice how the answer to both depends completely on Holy Spirit activity.

1) Spirit-empowered ministry. Paul says to pray that he will have the ability to make the good news about Jesus clear to people. The gospel is so mysterious, difficult for the unregenerate to understand, he says. He needs Holy Spirit empowerment to proclaim the Word with life-transforming effect.

2) Spirit-empowered life. In the parallel passage in his letter to the church in Ephesus, Paul asks more than once that they pray for his boldness (Eph 6:19-20). And in the Colossians passage he tells us that Epaphras "is always wrestling in prayer for you, that you may stand firm in all the will of God, mature and fully assured" (Col 4:12). Persistent warfare for holy living in the power of the Spirit. What Paul tells the believers to do is a fine outline of what prayer for the missionary should include: "Be wise in the way you act toward outsiders; make the most of every opportunity. Let your conversation be always full of grace,

seasoned with salt, so that you may know how to answer everyone" (Col 4:5-6).

Thus prayer is the secret to Spirit empowerment of the missionary enterprise, to give the gifts needed to proclaim the gospel and the fruit needed to demonstrate the gospel.

As we address the role of the Holy Spirit in missions, we must begin with the clear teaching of Scripture on the eight indispensable activities of the Spirit, reminding one another constantly that the mission is his, not ours. And we must link up with Holy Spirit power through prayer warfare, *strategic* for the whole cause and *tactical* for the missionaries we are responsible for, continuing in prayer that the Spirit will energize their ministry and empower their lives. Let us stop playing church, sleeping through traditional routines, guarding our own special formula or—worse—our own private turf, or chasing after the latest innovation. Let us rather turn godward and expect the Spirit himself to win out in our day, in the churches and in the world.

3

CONFIDENCE IN THE SPIRIT AS THE GOVERN-
ING ETHOS OF THE PAULINE MISSION

Don N. Howell, Jr.

Introduction: Roland Allen Still Speaks

More than 80 years have passed since the Anglican missionary-statesman Roland Allen wrote his classic work contrasting the mission methodology of his day with that of the apostle Paul.[1] In Part I Allen establishes the permanent relevance of Paul's model of church planting by refuting contentions that the apostle faced a unique set of moral and social conditions that no longer apply in the complex modern world. In Part II Allen identifies the principles of finance that Paul employed to promote and preserve the integrity of his evangelistic work, and the contextualized, decision-oriented manner in which he proclaimed the gospel. It is in Parts III and IV that Allen tackles the thorny issues surrounding the training of converts (III) and the gathering of converts into organized churches (IV). It is here that he makes his most distinctive contribution.

Though many of his illustrations, drawn mainly from Anglican work in China in the early years of this century, are dated, his criticism of paternalistic missionary approaches to the training of believers and the development of churches remains all too painfully true as we approach the 21st century. Running as a subtheme throughout Allen's work is the

---

[1]Roland Allen, *Missionary Methods: St. Paul's or Ours?* Reprint of 2nd ed., 1927 (Grand Rapids: Eerdmans, 1962). First edition was 1912.

centrality of the Holy Spirit in any effective missionary endeavor. Allen believed that the missionaries of his day lacked confidence in the Holy Spirit to build the church through Word and sacrament. This was in marked contrast with the apostle Paul who demonstrated a deep-seated confidence in the Holy Spirit to guide, preserve and pastor the church during his sustained absence. Several of Allen's most insightful observations follow:

1. Paul was not afraid to call out and endorse (though with qualification, cf. 1 Cor 14) the prophetic and didactic capacities of local believers even though risks were involved in "unstable" churches such as the one at Corinth. The simplicity and brevity with which he taught his converts the foundational elements of the faith stimulated the believers to dependence on the Spirit to live out their faith and apply biblical principles to their local contexts.[2]

2. Paul's practice was to administer baptism immediately upon genuine repentance, faith, and confession of Jesus as Lord (Acts 16:33). However, after leaving a place, he committed the governance of the church into the hands of the local leaders to decide how and when to admit others into the community of faith (1 Cor 1:14-17). Thus he avoided the opposite extremes of being too hasty or too protracted in permitting baptism. He neither required a drawn out pre-baptismal catechetical training before administering the initiatory sacrament (which, Allen believes, is a major hindrance to church growth) nor interfered with the appointed church leaders in screening baptismal candidates

[2]Ibid., 90-94.

after his departure. Local believers would have more understanding of the spiritual condition of their fellow citizens among whom they lived and worked than he would from a distance. He trusted the Spirit to guide the leaders in their oversight of the church.[3]

3. While Paul defended and exercised his apostolic authority over the churches, especially in the volatile Galatian (Gal 1:10-2:21) and Corinthian situations (1 Cor 7:17; 11:16, 34; 2 Cor 10:8; 13:10), he dealt with problems in the churches not by decree but by setting forth theological principles which the believers should have the maturity to discern and apply. One is especially impressed here by the manner in which Paul addressed the vexing moral and relational problems that disturbed the church in Corinth: fornication (1 Cor 6:13-19; cf. 1 Thess 4:1-8); litigation (1 Cor 6:1-11); participation in temple banquets and eating of meat offered to idols (1 Cor 8:1-13; 10:14-22); and marriage and divorce, where he distinguishes his advice from dominical tradition (1 Cor 7:6, 10, 12, 25, 40). Like Jesus, Paul inculcated principles and left the believers to apply them in their local settings. This was a stimulus to responsible and mature decision making via the exercise of moral discretion (Phil 3:15; cf. Heb 5:14). His *modus operandi* was not to lord it over their faith but to stand alongside the believers as a helper, confident they were standing firm in their faith (2 Cor 1:24; cf. Phil 1:6).[4]

---

[3]Ibid., 95-99.
[4]Ibid., 111-25.

In summary, Allen calls missionaries and mission agencies to recover the apostle's bedrock conviction that the Spirit dwells in the church to convict, correct, guide and fortify her.[5] This does not mean the missionary's abdication of prayerful concern for and ongoing pastoral communication to freshly planted churches. Such conviction, however, will translate into willing retirement and withdrawal accompanied by gradual and real handover of responsibility to the local leadership.[6] Does the evidence available bear the weight of this thesis that the governing ethos of Paul's church planting mission was his confidence in the Spirit? We believe it does. Recent scholarship has focused attention on the social setting of the first century Pauline churches and the psychological dynamics that moved the mind of the apostle himself.[7] Yet with all the rich insights gained from such research, there is the danger that the underlying theological truths which determined Paul's response to emergent issues—transcendant of social conditioning and psychological mechanisms—should be overlooked. Paul, the Spirit-directed theologian-missionary, is then transformed into an anthropologist, social therapist and/or itinerant philosopher. For Paul it was the empowering presence of the Spirit of God that gave to this new covenant ministry its glorious character (2 Cor 3:7-18). The corporate church was the temple of the Spirit (1 Cor 3:16-17). In the following representa-

---

[5]Ibid., 148-54.

[6]Dean S. Gilliland, *Pauline Theology and Mission Practice* (Grand Rapids: Baker, 1983) is in many ways an updating and expansion of Allen's work. Gilliland draws heavily on Allen's works (see pp. 41-45, 123-25, 154, 157, 188-89, 199, 200-2, 217-19, 243-46, 247-48, 251, 271, 273, 277, 285, 286) and similarly stresses the centrality of the Spirit in every phase of church planting (pp. 44-45, 108-9, 124-43, 156-57, 187-90, 201-4).

[7]A helpful summary of the literature is S. C. Barton, "Social-Scientific Approaches to Paul," in *DPHL*, 892-900.

tive look at the evidence we hope to show that the Spirit's presence in the church was for the apostle Paul a truth that conditioned every dimension of his ministry.

The Church in Thessalonica[8]

An early test of Paul's confidence in God to preserve the church came in Macedonia on the second missionary journey. After an encouraging start brought infant churches into being in Philippi, Thessalonica, and Berea the apostle was prematurely prevented by persecution from continuing his discipling of young believers (Acts 16:40; 17:9-10, 13-15). Yet in Paul's extended absence the fledgling groups in Philippi and Thessalonica matured into exemplary churches marked respectively by sacrificial giving and missionary zeal (Phil 1:5-6; 4:10-19; 1 Thess 1:7-8). The results in Thessalonica are particularly impressive since Paul spent at most two to three months and possibly much less from the time he initially entered the city until he was driven out.[9] Paul later

---

[8]The following are the major commentaries on the Thessalonian epistles cited in this paper: F. F. Bruce, *1 & 2 Thessalonians* WBC 45 (Waco, TX: Word, 1982); James E. Frame, *A Critical and Exegetical Commentary on the Epistles of St. Paul to the Thessalonians* ICC (Edinburgh: T. & T. Clark, 1912); D. Edmond Hiebert, *The Thessalonian Epistles: A Call to Readiness* (Chicago: Moody, 1971); Charles A. Wanamaker, *The Epistles to the Thessalonians* NIGTC (Grand Rapids: Eerdmans, 1990).

[9]Acts 17:2 records Paul preaching in the synagogue on three consecutive Sabbaths. His total time in the city was probably longer since he developed such an intimate relationship with the believers (1 Thess 2:7-11) and repeated gifts came from Philippi to support his work there (Phil 4:16). Still, the misunderstanding over his eschatological teaching (1 Thess 4:13-5:11; 2 Thess 2:1-12) is evidence that his stay was cut short while the church was still in an embryonic state. Actually, the stay in Philippi may not have been much

writes (from Corinth in early summer, perhaps four or five months after leaving Thessalonica)[10] that he was "torn away" from them in person, not in thought, and despite every effort to return has been hindered by Satan (1 Thess 2:17-18). In fact, Paul would not make his way again to Macedonia until the latter part of his third missionary journey, after leaving Ephesus and en route to Corinth (Acts 20:1-2).[11] What was intended to be a "short time" (1 Thess 2:17) turned into a 5 1/2 year separation. Yet God by his Spirit preserved his church so that Paul, on the eve of his visit to deliver the gifts of the Gentile churches to the impoverished brethren in Judea, could praise the churches of Macedonia as being willing and sacrificial participants in that offering (2 Cor 8:1-5).[12]

How is it that such an effective church planting work could be accomplished in such a short period of time with such limited direct missionary involvement and follow up? While it would not be wise to extrapolate a universal paradigm from first century Thessalonica (the cultural obstacles and spiritual resistance to planting an indigenous church

---

longer since the events surrounding the earthquake shortened what could have been a lengthy incarceration and trial.

[10]The unpublished chronology of H. Hoehner (Th.D. Dissertation, Dallas Theological Seminary, revised 1972) places Paul in Thessalonica from November 50 until January 51. 1 and 2 Thessalonians are written from Corinth in that order and separated by a few weeks in summer 51. This chronology is based on an A.D. 33 date for the death of Jesus.

[11]According to Hoehner, Paul arrived in Macedonia the first of June 56 and left Macedonia the middle of November 56, arriving in Corinth the end of November.

[12]Acts 20:4 lists seven men who are almost certainly the delegates appointed to accompany Paul to Jerusalem and deliver the funds collected from their respective churches (cf. 2 Cor 8:23-24). Of the seven listed, three are from Macedonia (one Berean, Sopater, and two Thessalonians, Aristarchus and Secundus).

among the Budddhists of Central Thailand or the Uyghur Muslims of N.W. China, for example, are much greater), we concur with Allen, Gilliland, and others that the apostle's dependence on and confidence in the work of the Holy Spirit at every level of the church building endeavor was the essential factor that gave the work its dynamic staying power. Even in this so-called enlightened day of missiological depth and sophistication there often exists a hidden and subtle form of paternalism born out of an anemia of assurance that the Spirit is both able and committed to guide, preserve, and perfect the church which he indwells.

The Spirit at Work in Thessalonica

We begin by looking carefully at the explicit references Paul makes to the Spirit in the Thessalonian correspondence, drawing heavily on the magisterial work on Pauline pneumatology by Gordon Fee.[13] Paul employs the term *pneu'ma* only eight times in 1 and 2 Thessalonians (1 Thess 1:5, 6; 4:8; 5:19, 23; 2 Thess 2:2, 8, 13). Of these, once it is translated "breath" (2 Thess 2:8), once it refers to the human spirit (1 Thess 5:23), and once to a prophetic utterance (2 Thess 2:2). It would be grossly inaccurate to conclude, however, that the five remaining explicit references to the Spirit exhaust the Spirit-language of these letters. There is much more here than meets the eye.

1. 1 Thessalonians 1:5-6

After saluting the believers, the apostle launches into his characteristic thanksgiving for the church. He remembers

---

[13]Gordon D. Fee, *God's Empowering Presence: The Holy Spirit in the Letters of Paul* (Peabody, MS: Hendrickson, 1994), 39-80.

the concrete demonstrations of their faith, hope, and love he observed while among them (1:3-4). Then comes a bold declaration of their election as God's beloved people (1:4), an election evidenced[14] by their conversion when they responded in a Spirit-originated joy to the Spirit-empowered preaching of the gospel (1:5-6). Both the initial proclamation of the Word of God in Thessalonica (1:5) and their joyful response at hearing the message (1:6) were Spirit-inspired.[15]

Two dimensions of the Spirit's centrality in the pioneer stages of this new church plant are identified. First, the effectiveness of the preaching as it penetrated the hearts of the listeners ("it came to you in . . . "), rather than the manner in which it was proclaimed, is traced to the Spirit.[16] The Spirit powerfully drove home the truth of the message to the minds and consciences of the listeners, producing deep con-

---

[14]We take the *oʃti* that introduces v. 5 as epexegetical rather than causal (contra NIV). If causal, then vv. 5-6 provide the ground of Paul's assurance in v. 4. Either way, the confidence of Paul emerges from the effectual work of the Spirit in the Thessalonians' lives.

[15]The content of the message can be reconstructed from 1 Thess 9-10: (i) the essential difference between idols and the one true and living God (theology proper); (ii) the death and resurrection of Jesus , the Son of God (Christology); (iii) the return of Jesus to judge (God's wrath) unbelievers and rescue his people (soteriology/ eschatology); and (iv) an appeal to "turn" (repentance) from idols and to "serve" (faith/obedience) the living God.

[16]Fee, *God's Empowering Presence*, 44-45. He cites this as the majority view among commentators, including Ellicott, Lightfoot, Frame, Moffatt, Whiteley, Hendriksen, Best, Morris, Hiebert, O'Brien, Marshall, and Dunn (f.n. 29). It is possible that we have here another all too familiar false dichotomy; perhaps the language refers to the powerful Spirit-produced conviction in which the apostles delivered their message *and* in which it was received by the Thessalonians.

viction or full assurance (1:5).[17] These believers embraced the apostolic word with their entire personalities from the outset. Second, the ability of the believers to experience such joyful reception of the Word even in much affliction originated in the work of the Spirit. In so doing they became imitators of the Lord Jesus and the apostles who similarly experienced joy in suffering (1:6). Deep conviction and unrestrained joy, then, were the hallmarks of the Spirit's work in their lives at the initial proclamation of the gospel. The apostle's assurance in the positional reality of the Thessalonians' election by God emerges from his firsthand observation of their personal, experiential appropriation of the Word of God. The Spirit is everywhere in the genesis of this new community of God![18]

2. 1 Thessalonians 4:8

Paul's belief in a new community endowed with the Spirit does not mean that its obedience to the Spirit is automatic. Paraenesis or ethical instruction backed up by apostolic authority was central to his ministry when among them

---

[17]The Greek word is *plhroforiva*. Elsewhere in the New Testament both this noun (Col 2:2; Heb 6:11; 10:22) and its cognate verb *plhroforevw* (Rom 4:21; 14:5; 15:13 Col 4:12) refer to the full assurance or deep confidence that believers possess in God's person and promises.

[18]This is true not only with respect to the exemplary Thessalonian church but also to the troubled Galatian and Corinthian congregations where the apostle also reminds the believers of their vivid initial experience of the Spirit when they were converted under the proclamation of the gospel (Gal 3:1-3; 1 Cor 2:4-5). Behind the severe admonitory tones of the Galatian and Corinthian correspondence is an underlying confidence in the Spirit's involvement with these congregations whom he addresses as "brothers" (Gal 1:11; 3:15; 4:12, 28, 31; 5:11, 13; 6:1, 18) and "saints" (1 Cor 1:2; 2 Cor 1:1).

and is followed up with detail in his letters (1 Thess 4:1-2). M. B. Thompson identifies three formative factors that shaped Paul's moral teachings to the churches: an awareness of Christian freedom in the Spirit, the mandate of Christian witness to the world, and the character of Christ demonstrated preeminently in the cross.[19] The paraenetic material in 1 Thessalonians 4:1-5:23 shares this framework: the Holy Spirit strives with God's people to produce in them moral purity (4:8; 5:23) and unbounded joy, prayer, and thanksgiving (5:16-18); vital Christian living will commend the gospel to outsiders who observe the Christians' love for one another and their diligence in work (4:9-12);[20] and salvation secured by the death and resurrection of Jesus is the indicative reality in which these ethical imperatives are grounded (4:14; 5:9-10).

The low moral standards of first century Greco-Roman culture, particularly with regard to sexual intercourse before and outside of marriage (*porneiva*), exerted a powerful influence on the church.[21] It was not enough to call the church to the avoidance of all sexual activity outside of marriage and to honorable self-control over one's body[22]—both

---

[19]M. B. Thompson, "Teaching/Paraenesis," in *Dictionary of Paul and His Letters* (abbrev. DPHL), eds. Gerald F. Hawthorne, Ralph P. Martin (Downers Grove, IL: InterVarsity, 1993), 923.

[20]P. H. Towner, *The Goal of Our Instruction: The Structure of Theology and Ethics in the Pastoral Epistles* JSNT Sup 34 (Sheffield: JSOT Press, 1989), demonstrates that the theology and paraenesis of the Pastoral Epistles is to promote the church's mission of commending the gospel to the surrounding community.

[21]W. A. Meeks, *The Moral World of the First Christians* (Philadelphia: Westminster, 1986); *TDNT*, VI: 579-84.

[22]The term *skeu'o"* (translated "body" in the NIV) is taken by many as a metaphor for "wife." But the obscurity (why not use the word *gunhv* as he does elsewhere [cf. 1 Cor 7:3-4, 27] ?) and questionable contextual fit (what does a command to keep or acquire [*ktavomai*] a

of which Paul did without compromise (4:3-4). The appeal must be supported by the requisite spiritual resources to enable obedience. It is for the maintenance of such purity, Paul says, that God gives to believers his Holy Spirit (4:7-8). Fee draws out from this teaching four implications regarding Paul's understanding of the Spirit:[23] (i) the designation "Holy Spirit" has a functional dimension to it: the Spirit is himself holy and communicates God's holiness to his people;[24] (ii) the Spirit is not given as an external force moving the believer from without but indwells the believer transforming him/her from within;[25] (iii) the Spirit is viewed as "the constant divine companion" whose presence and power is continuously supplied;[26] and (iv) the Spirit is the energizing force that makes victory over sexual temptation and the control over one's sex drive a possibility (cf. Rom 8:4-12). Sandwiched between the instruction (4:3-4) and the source of enablement (4:7-8) is a comparison and a warning of judgment (4:5-6): the pure church must stand in stark contrast to heathen society characterized by dishonorable passions which, acted out, injure and defraud the victims and in turn invite God's judgment. Those in Thessalonica yearning for relief from the downward spiral of sexual abuse

---

wife in holiness and honor have to do with concern about sexual immorality [v. 3b] or unrestrained passion [v. 5]?) of such a meaning weighs against it. We concur with Wanamaker, 152: *skeu'o"* here connotes "the human body in its sexual aspect, that is, a euphemism for the genitalia."

[23]Fee, *God's Empowering Presence*, 51-53.

[24]"Holiness" language permeates this paragraph and establishes the connection: *aJgiavsmo"* (vv. 3, 4, 7) and to; *a{gion* (v. 8).

[25]The phrase *eij" uJma'"* is reminiscent of LXX Ezek 37:6, 14 where the new covenant provision of an indwelling Spirit is promised.

[26]The durative, continuous force of the present participle *to;n didovnta* should be retained (cf. Gal 3:5, *oJ ejpicorhgw'n*).

and exploitation will be attracted to the honorable conduct of these Christians. Their self-control, faith, love, and hope will shine as lights in the community and roll back the darkness (1 Thess 5:4-11). Does the apostle, then, not create a powerful fusion between Spirit and mission in his paraenesis?

3. 1 Thessalonians 5:16-24

Couched in the middle of a series of eight rapid-fire imperatives (5:16-22) is the command, "Do not quench the Spirit" (5:19). The three preceding imperatives relate to the spiritual character and lifestyle of believers—continual rejoicing, unceasing prayer, and thanksgiving in all situations (5:16-18). The four commands that follow relate to the corporate worship of the church, particularly its posture toward prophetic utterances in the assembly (5:19-21). Most commentators relate the prohibition not to quench the Spirit exclusively to the commands that follow, that is, the Spirit is suppressed[27] when the church proscribes, for whatever reason, "charismatic manifestations" in the church, such as prophecy.[28] "To quench, to put out the fire of, the Spirit is to prohibit or repress those who *ejn pneuvmati* are ready with psalm, teaching, revelation, tongue, interpretation, etc. (1 Cor 14:26)."[29] The connection of v. 19 with what follows is unmistakable. The spiritual energy created by the Spirit as believers exercise their spiritual gifts to the edification of the

---

[27]The Greek word *sbevnnumi* is used elsewhere in the New Testament of the literal extinguishing of fire (Mk 9:48; Mt 25:8; Heb 11:34) and figuratively in Mt 12:20; Eph 6:16. Here the meaning approximates "suppress" or "impede." The Spirit is associated with fire on the Day of Pentecost as a symbol of the divine presence (Acts 2:3; cf. Exod 3:2; Heb 12:29).

[28]Fee, *God's Empowering Presence, 58-59.*

[29]Frame, *Epistles to the Thessalonians,* 205.

whole is a flame to be fanned, not quenched.[30] But the cautionary words that follow in vv. 21-22 bring balance to what precedes: openness to the charismatic manifestations of the Spirit must be combined with vigilance to test the genuineness of the utterance as to its conformity to apostolic tradition (2 Thess 2:15) and the canon of edification (1 Cor 14:3). Any individual prophetic utterance or other charismatic manifestation that does not conform to apostolic teaching or is divisive rather than edifying is an "evil kind" of expression which is not of the Spirit and must be avoided.[31]

The apostle Paul's antidote to charismatic excesses in the church is not disuse of spiritual gifts but correction of abuse. Here we encounter Paul's characteristic respect for a very young congregation's ability to monitor its own life and worship. Fear of abuse does not drive Paul to legislating or micromanaging the conduct of the Thessalonians with a myriad of apodictic ("you shall/shall not . . .") or casuistic ("if[or whoever] . . . , then . . .") laws. He simply urges them to apply their Christian minds in testing all things, believing that they have both the capacity and will to do so. If anything, he is more concerned that the exercise of their spiritual gifts in an open and free atmosphere not be choked off by

---

[30]Bruce, *1 & 2 Thessalonians*, 125, recalls the attempt of Jeremiah to speak no more in Yahweh's name but the word held back became "in my heart like a fire shut up in my bones" which could not be quenched or tamed (Jer 20:9). Old Testament examples of quenching the Spirit would include Joshua's attempt to shut up Eldad and Medad from prophesying in the Spirit (Num 11:26-30), the Israelites' command that the prophets cease to prophesy (Amos 2:12), and the false prophets of Micah's day demand that God's true prophet quit his prophecies of judgment (Micah 2:6).

[31]Fee, *God's Empowering Presence*, 61-62. Such charismatic excesses would break out in full at Corinth and are addressed at length by the apostle in 1 Corinthians 12-14.

the timid and the uncomfortable souls around them.[32] A fire can be controlled but the cold ashes of once flaming embers that were constantly doused with the waters of fear and suspicion can only be swept away. The apostle was not afraid of the principles of grace and liberty because he believed the indwelling Spirit, if allowed to govern without hindrance, would pastor and perfect the church.

The command not to quench the Spirit, however, may well condition the imperatives that precede it (5:16-18) as much as it does those that follow. This is made probable by the fact that elsewhere in the New Testament the actions of rejoicing, prayer, and thanksgiving are attributed to the work of the indwelling Spirit. Joy translated into rejoicing is a mark of the Spirit's presence (Acts 13:52; 1 Thess 1:6; Gal 5:22; Rom 14:17; 15:13). Prayer is an activity undergirded by the Spirit of God (1 Cor 14:15; Rom 8:26-27; Eph 6:18), of which supplication and thanksgiving are an integral part (Phil 4:6-7). Unhindered joy and unceasing prayer with thanksgiving are burning embers lit by the fire of the Spirit and must be fanned, not quenched, just as much as the exercise of *carismavta* in corporate worship. D. E. Hiebert captures the broader meaning of 1 Thess 5:19: "The Spirit's fire is quenched whenever His presence is ignored and His promptings are suppressed or rejected, or the fervor which he kindles in the heart are dampened by unspiritual attitudes, criticisms, or actions."[33]

---

[32]The present imperatives of vv. 19-20 (with the negative *mhv*) should be translated with their normal durative sense: "no longer quench/despise." Apparently the quenching and despising was already taking place and Paul wants it to stop.

[33]Hiebert, *The Thessalonian Epistles*, 244. A similar expression occurs in Romans 12:11, "not lacking in zeal, boiling in the Spirit, serving the Lord." Fee (*God's Empowering Presence*, 611-13) renders *tw'l pneuvmati zevonte*" in his characteristic dual manner: "fervent in Spirit/spirit." In this understanding Paul refers to both the fervency

The commands are followed by a prayer for the God of peace to sanctify the church (pl. "you," "your") in preparation for the return of the Lord Jesus Christ (5:23-24). Though the Spirit is not referred to explicitly, his work is implied in God the Father's sanctifying work. In 4:7-8 it is the Holy Spirit who is given by God to enable the believer to grow in holiness. Further, Paul speaks elsewhere of the human spirit as the locus of the Spirit's work in the human personality (Rom 8:16). Here *pneu'ma* is the first of a three part description for the personality which also includes the body.[34] The composite expression indicates the comprehensive nature of God's sanctifying work. The apostle prays with confident faith that God will by his Spirit continue to sanctify believers in preparation for the return of Christ. Such confidence reaches its zenith when Paul projects himself into the future and contemplates the joy he will experience when his spiritual children are ushered into the Lord's presence at his return (1 Thess 2:19-20).

4. 2 Thessalonians 1:11

Once again Paul contemplates the glorification of believers at the time of Christ's return (1:10). To this very end Paul then prays that God "by his power" (*ejn dunavmei*) will (i) make them worthy of his calling by lives that conform to that call, and (ii) bring to fulfillment every desire for good-

---

that the Spirit provides for service and to the locus of this work of the Spirit, namely, the human spirit. His justification for such an inclusive translation on other passages (1 Cor 5:3, 4; 6:17; 14:14, 15; Col 2:5) is found on pp. 24-26.

[34]Fee, *God's Empowering Presence*, 15 (n. 6), lists this as one of fourteen passages in Paul that refer exclusively to the human spirit (1 Thess 5:23; 1 Cor 2:11; 5:5; 7:34; 14:14; 16:18; 2 Cor 2:13; 7:13; Gal 6:18; Rom 1:9; 8:16; Phlm 25; Phil 4:23; 2 Tim 4:22).

ness and every act that is prompted by their faith.[35] Paul probably uses *ejn dunavmei* as a shorthand expression for the power of God's Spirit (as in 1 Thess 1:5). In Galatians 5:22 both faith (*pivsti"*) and goodness (*ajgaqwsuvnh*) are part of the ninefold fruit of the Spirit. Here their pursuit of goodness and faith-inspired action are grounded in the effective work of God by his Spirit.

5. 2 Thessalonians 2:1-2

G. Fee labels this passage as "at once the most crucial and most problematic in the letter."[36] Paul is anxious to correct the false teaching that had entered the church, and had actually been accepted by some, that the Day of the Lord has in some sense already arrived. Perhaps this was in part related to a wrong understanding of 1 Thessalonians 5:1-11 where Paul predicted that many will be caught completely unprepared when the Lord suddenly returns "like a thief in the night" (5:2). What form this alien teaching took is uncertain but Paul counters that several antecedent events must take place before the Day of the Lord—his final return to judge unbelievers and gather his elect—will arrive (2 Thess 2:3-12).

The means by which the false teaching was communicated is identified as "some prophecy, report or letter supposed to have come from us" (2 Thess 2:2, NIV).[37] Paul

---

[35]Such a rendering takes *ajgaqwsuvnh"* as an objective genitive (NIV renders as a Semitic or adjectival genitive: "every good purpose") and *pivstew"* as a subjective genitive or genitive of origin.

[36]Fee, *God's Empowering Presence*, 71.

[37]We follow the usual way of rendering the final phrase, *wJ" diΔ hJmw'n*, as modifying all three preceding words. Fee, *God's Empowering Presence*, 73-74, sees the sentence as elliptical with *wJ" diΔ hJmw'n* introducing the clause content that follows. Either way, the doctrine in error is being attributed to Paul by those trying to

is aware that this false teaching has been attributed to him by those who endorsed it but he is uncertain whether it came through a prophetic utterance (simply *pneuvmato"* in the Greek), a verbal report, or a written forgery. Paul had previously instructed them both by word of mouth and by letter (2:15). Any other communications purportedly from him which contradict his earlier teaching must be steadfastly rejected. Here is another call for the church to test prophetic utterances, and all communications, in light of apostolic tradition (cf. 1 Thess 5:19-22). In fact, 2 Thessalonians 2:15 provides the criterion by which prophetic declarations in the assembly can be tested to determine whether they are really from the Spirit, namely, "the traditions you were taught whether by word of mouth or by letter." Paul will not discourage the church's freedom to exercise the full array of spiritual gifts even when one of them, the gift of prophecy, is exploited by ignorant or perhaps even malicious individuals to disturb the church with errant doctrine. He delegates to the church the task of weighing prophetic utterances and other communications according to the sound traditions he has delivered to them. Freedom with responsibility, he knows well, is just the mix that will produce a healthy and mature church.

6. 2 Thessalonians 2:13

The main antecedent event that must precede the Day of the Lord is the revelation of "the man of lawlessness" (2:3) or "the lawless one" (2:8). This individual will display miraculous signs and wonders which originate in Satan's effective working to counterfeit God's supernatural miracles (2:9). The same phenomena that accompanied the apostolic preaching to authenticate its truthfulness (Rom 15:19; 2 Cor 12:12), namely, "signs and wonders" wrought

---

influence the church.

by the Spirit of God, here arise from the spirit of Satan and are intended to deceive. Fee comments that this may well explain why Paul is reluctant to bring forward his apostolic "signs and wonders and miracles" (2 Cor 12:12) as the definitive mark of his authentication when he defends himself against the attacks of the false apostles in 2 Corinthians 10-13: "For him the evidence of apostleship lies ultimately not in the miraculous—in the sense of 'signs and wonders,' since Satan can also produce these—but in his own 'imitation of Christ' in his sufferings and in the fruit of such imitation, the conversion of the Corinthians themselves."[38]

Many will be led astray by the miraculous works of this evil personage (2:9-11). But the apostle is confident that the Thessalonians are not among them, for God elected them to salvation, evidenced by their belief in the truth and the sanctifying work of the Spirit (2:13). Once again the Spirit is associated with holiness communicated to believers (cf. 1 Thess 4:7-8; 5:23). This is positional sanctification or "setting apart" of believers as God's holy people which takes place at conversion (cf. Rom 15:16; 1 Cor 1:2, 30; 6:11) and which is designed to issue in personal and experiential holiness also produced by the indwelling Spirit (1 Thess 4:8). God has inaugurated his good work of salvation in these believers by the effectual work of his Spirit and is continuing by the same Spirit to perfect them. This is the ground of Paul's thanksgiving for them, even as he contemplates the ominous events that await fulfillment on the stage of human history (2 Thess 2:1-12). Warning, command, prohibition, exhortation, prayer, and thanks-giving all find their place within an overall atmosphere of assurance that these are God's Spirit-people whose present and future is secure in his redemptive purposes.

---

[38]Ibid., 76-77.

Summary of the Pneumatology
of the Thessalonian Epistles

Though the explicit references to the Holy Spirit are few in number, they are comprehensive in scope. *First,* the power of the Holy Spirit, which accompanied the initial proclamation of the gospel by the apostolic team in Thessalonica, brought deep conviction (1 Thess 1:5). Even though resistance was fierce, the Spirit made the apostolic visit result in a successful beginning (1 Thess 2:1-2). *Second,* the conversion of these people was wrought by the same Spirit. He brought them first to deep conviction of sin followed by a joyous response to the promise of forgiveness (1 Thess 1:5-6). The Spirit set them apart as God's holy people when they believed the truth (2 Thess 2:13). *Third,* their ongoing Christian experience and growth is everywhere seen as Spirit-led: holiness in personal morality (1 Thess 4:8); joy, prayer and thanksgiving (1 Thess 5:16-18); the desire to do God's good will; and actions that spring from faith (2 Thess 1:11). *Fourth,* the wise exercise of spiritual gifts in the assembly, especially prophecy, is a manifestation of the Spirit flaming among them and must not be quenched (1 Thess 5:19-22; 2 Thess 2:1-2). Paul believes that the Spirit has been intimately involved on every level of the church planting endeavor in the Macedonian capital. He is certain that even in his forced and extended absence the same Spirit will preserve, strengthen, and perfect this young church.

Apostolic Parousia and Team Ministry

R. W. Funk identified literary units in the undisputed Pauline letters on the basis of their form and content and labeled them "apostolic parousia" passages.[39] The apostle

---

[39]R. W. Funk, "The Apostolic Parousia: Form and Signifi-

in these passages makes his presence and authority felt by expressing his pastoral concern for the church, his anxious plans to visit at the first opportunity, and the more immediate visit of an envoy in his place. "The letter and the envoy are anticipatory substitutes for Paul's own personal presence when he cannot travel, but both function as a means of conveying his apostolic presence."[40] This balances the thesis of R. Allen (which we cited earlier) that Paul practiced conscious retirement from his churches in order to allow them the freedom to develop their own patterns of life and worship under local leaders. In Thessalonica and elsewhere his withdrawal was sometimes necessitated by persecution and his letters are intended to be his pastoral voice to areas of the church still lacking. Even here, though, Paul is reluctant to rule by apostolic decree but rather challenges the church to direct its own affairs within the parameters of sound apostolic tradition. The trust he places in his emissaries once again reveals his deep confidence in the Spirit to guide the ongoing life of the church through members of his missionary team.

The central section of 1 Thessalonians, 2:17-3:13, falls into this category of apostolic parousia. Paul writes of his "intense longing" to see these from whom he has been prematurely "torn away" (2:17). In his place he sent Timothy to strengthen and encourage their faith in the midst of trials and persecutions (3:2-3). In his heart is a mixture of assurance and anxiety: assurance that these believers will be gloriously perfected at the return of Christ (2:19-20); anxiety that the tempter might undermine their faith and his efforts

---

cance," in *Christian History and Interpretation: Studies Presented to John Knox* , ed. W. R. Farmer, C. F. D. Moule and R. R. Niebuhr (Cambridge: University Press, 1967), 249-68.

[40]P. Trebilco, "Itineraries, Travel Plans, Journeys, Apostolic Parousia," *DPHL*, 449.

prove vain (3:5).[41] But Timothy's mission to Thessalonica was a success and he has now returned to Paul in Corinth with a thrilling report of their faith, love, and loyalty which fills the apostle with prayerful thanksgiving (3:6-10). At this point it is helpful to summarize Paul's contact with the Thessalonian church between his forced departure and subsequent writing of this epistle from Corinth:

1. Paul's brief ministry in Thessalonica was cut short by Jewish persecution and he fled with Silas to Berea (Acts 17:10). Timothy is not mentioned in Acts 17:10 and perhaps stayed in Thessalonica or returned to Philippi, but later joined Paul and Silas in Berea (Acts 17:14).

2. Paul is soon driven from Berea by these same Thessalonian Jews, leaving Silas and Timothy behind (Acts 17:14).

3. Coming to Athens he preaches in the synagogue and the marketplace, then addresses the Areopagus but finds minimal response (Acts 17:34). Alone in Athens, Paul sends for Silas and Timothy to come to him as soon as possible (Acts 17:15). Timothy joins Paul in Athens but is sent back to Thessalonica to stabilize the unsettled state of the church (1 Thess 3:1-5). Silas, not mentioned, may have moved to Philippi when Timothy returned to Thessalonica.

---

[41]Paul can live with such tensions. Many contemporary scholars, however, possess little tolerance for creative tension within the same author and thus find Paul to be a consistent source of frustration. See, for example, the portrait of Paul found in Leander E. Keck, "Images of Paul in the New Testament," *Interpretation* 43:4 (1989): 341-51.

4. Tired and discouraged (1 Cor 2:3), Paul moves on to Corinth. He is encouraged by the help of Priscilla and Aquila (Acts 18:1-3) and then by the arrival of Silas and Timothy from Macedonia (18:5). Timothy brings encouraging news of the church in Thessalonica (1 Thess 3:6) but also relates a number of concerns (perhaps contained in a letter) that Paul needs to address (*peri*; [*de*;]]]: 4:9, 13; 5:1). Paul responds by writing 1 Thessalonians as a pastoral letter.

Into the hands of young *Timothy*, then, Paul committed the pastoral aftercare of this vulnerable church. What an excellent choice it was and how clearly it demonstrates the wisdom of Paul's collaborative approach to ministry.[42] Timothy's pastoral ministry in both Thessalonica and Philippi (cf. Phil 2:19-24) proved to be a rich source of blessing to those churches and must in large part be due to the training he received from his apostle-mentor. Converted on Paul's first visit to Lystra (Acts 14:6-20) and added to the missionary team on his second visit there (Acts 16:1-3), Timothy was young both in faith and in ministry experience when he represented Paul to the churches in Macedonia.[43] Probably in his late teens at this time,[44] he was less than two years old in the Lord with only a few months experience in full-time missionary work. But Paul had seen the Spirit of

---

[42]D. J. Harrington, "Paul and Collaborative Ministry," *NTR* 3 (1990): 62-71.

[43]According to Hoehner (see footnote 10) the first visit to Lystra was March 49, the second visit in May 50, and the arrival in Macedonia in August 50.

[44] This is based on the fact that thirteen years later (approximate date of the writing of 1 Timothy, A. D. 62/63) Timothy is urged to let no one despise his "youth" (1 Tim 4:12, *neovth*").

God confirm God's call to Timothy and use the young man among the churches of Galatia. Less than a year after his conversion Timothy was commended by the brothers of Lystra and Iconium for his exemplary life and ministry among them (Acts 16:2). Then at the time of his ordination to missionary work the Spirit both gifted him for ministry and inspired several prophetic utterances that publicly confirmed his suitability for evangelistic and pastoral work (1 Tim 1:18; 4:14). Paul would trust the Spirit of God to use this servant to strengthen the church during his absence.

In fact, Paul's deep commitment to *team ministry* is another expression of his confidence in the Spirit. One of the keys to the success of Paul's mission was his ability to attract capable and dedicated men and women to work alongside him both in itinerant evangelism and in settled discipleship and follow up. It was a very diverse team of four that evangelized Macedonia: the battle-scarred veteran and converted Pharisee, Paul; the maturing leader and a Hellenistic Jewish believer from Jerusalem, Silas; the fresh recruit, half-Greek, half-Jew, Timothy; and the Greek layman, Luke, who joined the party at Troas (Acts 16:6-10). Here is solid biblical precedent for multi-cultural missionary teams demonstrating the unity of the Spirit in their proclamation of Jesus Christ, whose gospel transcends all such sociological barriers (Gal 3:28; Col 3:11).

E. Ellis lists the names of 36 coworkers that are referred to in Paul's letters under nine designations.[45] Of those

---

[45]E. E. Ellis, "Paul and His Coworkers," *DPHL*, 184. The Greek words of designation are: *ajdelfov"*, *ajpovstolo"* (in its nontechnical sense: Acts 14:4, 14; Rom 16:7; 1 Cor 4:9; Phil 2:25; 1 Thess 2:7), *diavkono"*, *(suvn)doulo"*, *koinwnov"*, *oJ kopiw'n*, *(su)stratiwvth"*, *sunaicmavlwto"*, *sunergov"*. D. Edmond Hiebert, *Personalities Around Paul* (Chicago: Moody, 1973) gathers the biblical data on eight "Prominent Personalities" and seventeen "Lesser Lights" who associated with Paul in ministry. In all, Hiebert cites 125 named

that were long-term coworkers, some were clearly subordinates (Erastus, Mark, Timothy, Titus, Tychicus), others maintained a cooperative but independent relationship to the Apostle (Apollos, Priscilla, and Aquila), and still others joined him only on specific missions (Barnabas, Silas).[46] Of greatest significance were those who had preaching and teaching gifts which Paul nurtured and utilized on behalf of the churches. In these Paul invested his energies, instructing them in apostolic *didachv* and *paravdosi*" and the Christological interpretation of the Old Testament (Rom 6:17; 16:17; 1 Cor 11:2; Gal 1:14; Col 2:8; 2 Thess 2:15; 3:6). Though his trust was at times betrayed (Demas being the 'outstanding' example: Col 4:14; Phlm 24; 2 Tim 4:10) he committed to these individuals the pastoral care of the young churches he had planted, believing that the Spirit would superintend the teaching of his coworkers and guide the church to maturity. Timothy (to the churches of Macedonia: 1 Thess 3:6-10; Philem 2:19-24) and Titus (to the church in Corinth: 2 Cor 2:12-13; 7:5-16; 8:16-24; 12:18) were special instruments of the Spirit that Paul dispatched on difficult and sensitive missions.[47] To the former he would

---

individuals in addition to many unnamed individuals in the Pauline corpus (pp. 223-38).

[46]Ellis, "Paul and His Coworkers," 183.

[47]Not all of these missions proved successful. After Paul wrote 1 Corinthians he dispatched Timothy to Corinth to follow up his letter and admonish those who were seeking to undermine his authority in the church (1 Cor 4:17; 16:10-11; cf. Acts 19:22). Evidently Timothy was forced to leave Corinth quickly without positive results. Paul then made his 'painful visit' to Corinth where he was opposed and insulted by the anti-Paul group led by their ringleader (2 Cor 2:1; 12:14, 21; 13:1-2; ringleader referred to in 2 Cor 2:5-11; 7:12). After his return to Ephesus the problem worsened. Rather than Timothy, this time Paul sent Titus (perhaps in light of Gal 2:3-5 Titus was a stronger personality than the self-effacing Timothy [cf. 1 Cor 16:10-11; 1 Tim 4:12; 2 Tim 1:7] and more suited for confronta-

commit the pastoral ministry of the strategic church in Ephesus (1 Tim 1:3) and to the latter the leadership of the newly
organized church in Crete (Titus 1:5).

The apostle commends the local administrators,
teachers, and preachers who assumed leadership roles in the
local congregations and urges the churches to submit to their
oversight (1 Cor 16:15-18; Gal 6:6; Phil 1:1; 4:2-3; 1 Thess
5:12-13). Though Paul is famous (or infamous) for his
statements about the subordination of women to male leadership in the church (1 Cor 11:3-16; 14:33-35; 1 Tim 2:11-15)
he commends in his letters a remarkable number of women
as highly valued coworkers. He identifies these women with
the same designations as his male associates in ministry as
they are similarly engaged in the ministries of teaching and
preaching (Rom 16:1-3, 6-7, 12-13, 15; Phil 4:2-3; Col 4:15;
Philem 2; cf. Acts 16:14-15, 40; 18:26).

F. F. Bruce captures the principal factor that drives
the apostle to train others and delegate vital ministry concerns to them: "In all these things, discipline, administration
and others, the presence and directive power of the Holy
Spirit were so real to Paul that he implies them even where
he does not explicitly mention them. If he did not trust his
converts, corporately or individually, to advance along the

---

tional situations) who carried Paul's 'severe letter' which is no
longer extant (2 Cor 2:3, 4, 9; 7:8-12). When Titus' expected return
from Corinth was delayed, Paul traveled anxiously to Troas, then to
Macedonia where he at last met Titus and received wonderful news
about the repentance and return of the church to its true apostle-
founder (2 Cor 2:12-13; 7:5-16; cf. Acts 19:21; 20:1-2). In 2 Corinthians
10-13, however, we learn of fresh troubles that then broke out in
Corinth from "pseudo-apostles" (2 Cor 11:13) or "super-apostles" (2
Cor 11:5; 12:11). No church weighed heavier on Paul or tested his
confidence in the Spirit to guide and perfect the church as did the
one in Corinth (cf. 2 Cor 7:16; 11:28).

lines he laid down for them, his 'ways in Christ' (1 Cor 4:17), he trusted the Holy Spirit to work in his converts."[48]

The Pauline Principle at Work in Japan

As Japan began to rebuild after the devastation of the Second World War, a fresh generation of pioneering church planting missionaries entered. Some of the greatest advances in church planting came from the interdenominational faith mission agencies who agreed among themselves to a flexible comity arrangement in line with Paul's policy of "not building on someone else's foundation" (Rom 15:20). The largest of these agencies in terms of personnel committed to direct church planting are: OMF, whose work is centered in the northern island of Hokkaido and Aomori prefecture in northern Honshu; SEND, whose churches are primarily in Yokohama, Saitama prefecture and western Tokyo; the German Liebenzelle mission, whose work is centered in the central and southern Kanto plain; and TEAM, whose churches are spread more widely but with a concentration of churches in Shikoku. This is not to overlook the significant contribution of many other denominational and independent missions throughout Japan, though the autonomy with which these agencies have established churches has created a rather fractured evangelical witness in a general population that is still 99% non-Christian.[49]

---

[48]F. F. Bruce, "Paul in Acts and Letters, " *DPHL*, 689.

[49]This is changing through the Japan Evangelical Missions Association (JEMA) which has brought the various evangelical agencies and individuals together into an association that sponsors a quarterly magazine (*Japan Harvest*), an annual Bible conference, and local workshops throughout the country on issues related to evangelism, church planting, and theological education in Japan.

The church planting endeavor of these interdenominational mission agencies over the past four decades could be divided into three stages paralleling the development of the human personality:

1. *Infancy*: As individuals were won to Christ and new churches brought into existence there was initially a large measure of dependence on the financial and personnel resources of the parent mission. Until the mid-1960's Japan was rebuilding its economy. Thus the ability of small groups of believers to rent or purchase a building, as well as support a national pastor, was limited. Besides, there was a dearth of trained national leaders, which created the need for the establishment of theological training centers such as Hokkaido Bible Institute, Japan Bible Seminary, and Tokyo Christian College (now University). The pioneering work endured many setbacks but there emerged a constellation of churches organized into indigenous associations with their own structures, yet with an ethos and outlook drawn from the parent mission which spawned them.

2. *Adolescence*: As the churches and their well-trained national leaders multiplied, the associations entered into a stage of increasing tension with the mission agencies to which they had historic ties. There was a desire to contextualize the gospel and church life more fully to the culture and life patterns of Japan, an aspiration to which missionaries were not always sensitive. In matters of theology, church polity, and style of worship there was a questioning of some of the parameters that had been placed upon them by the parent missions in the formative years: mode of baptism, role and authority of the pastor and the elder board, principles of tithing, lines of authority and accountability in cooperative church planting endeavors, and the use of spiritual gifts. In some cases the national church felt the mission agencies had been too rigid, saddling the church with Western norms that clashed with Japanese culture. In other cases the churches wanted more uniformity, organizational structure,

and lines of accountability than the missionaries had felt comfortable with. This writer can remember a period in Hokkaido when the biannual pastor-missionary conferences were filled with tension and striving (which by God's grace never degenerated into hostility and bitterness) rather than unity and cooperation. *Here was a test case for the mission leadership*: would it act to pressure the church association to conform to its way of organizing the church and meeting its expectations, or would it trust the Spirit of God to move the church from rebellious adolescence to mature adulthood? Happily, the latter prevailed as the mission leadership rested its confidence in God's Spirit to guide and pastor the growing churches, respecting the national leaders' right to develop their own structures without interference. In turn relationships were strengthened (loyalty [*chuseishin*], that marvelous Japanese character quality, was abundantly evidenced) as the churches and mission agencies entered into a new period of equality and mutuality.

3. *Adulthood*: The next step involved the recognition of the national church leaders that the power of evangelical witness in Japan was blunted by the fractured nature of the church. If there was doctrinal purity and unity on the essentials of the faith (Japanese evangelicals consider the inerrancy of Scripture to be a *sine qua non* of genuine Christian theology and are mystified at the disagreement among American evangelicals over this matter) there could be friendly disagreement and freedom on the nonessentials. The distinctive ethos and values gained from the parent mission need not be lost in this ecclesiastical unity. So there began in the early 1980's informal meetings of the leaders of national church associations spawned by OMF, TEAM, Liebenzelle Mission, and SEND to explore whether a nationwide association of evangelical churches might be a possibility. Over the next decade the slow move toward consensus took shape and in 1992 the Japan Evangelical Church Association (JECA) was officially established, bringing together over 150

churches from Hokkaido to Okinawa. Mission leaders, though perhaps initially fearful that some of the distinctive emphases and values they saw as important might be diluted, encouraged the move. The result is a much stronger united witness with greater financial and personnel resources to pour into cooperative church planting thrusts into the many unreached towns and villages. Like Paul, the mission leaders (despite mistakes and shortcomings) nurtured the emerging churches from infancy through the turbulent period of adolescence and on to adulthood like a caring mother (1 Thess 2:7) and an encouraging father (1 Thess 2:11). They were confident that the Spirit who had brought the churches into being would sustain and perfect them.

Conclusion

The apostle Paul's dependence on and confidence in the empowering presence of the Spirit of God can be seen at every level of his Gentile mission. In a wide-ranging article on the Pauline concept of mission, W. P. Bowers looks at the apostle's missionary activity before exploring his missionary thought.[50] In an otherwise penetrating analysis there is one glaring omission—scarcely a reference is made to the Spirit as the generative force of the Gentile mission. Bowers' conclusion is that it is Paul's eschatological self-understanding which is the theological matrix that conditions his concept of mission. "What has now already been made available at the end of time in the Messiah is to be made available by Paul himself in a geographically defined outreach to the nations, in fulfillment of the OT eschatological promises, and it is to be realized in representative communities which demonstrate the life of the new age."[51] But we must go deeper.

---

[50]W. P. Bowers, "Mission," *DPHL*, 608-19.

[51]Ibid., 618. This is essentially the same conclusion reached

What signaled the inauguration of the eschatological age to the apostles was the outpouring of the Spirit upon the church of both Jew and Gentile. The promised age of the Spirit had begun now that Jesus had taken his lordly position at the right hand of the Father in fulfillment of Psalm 110:1. The exalted Lord Jesus was now mediating his presence to his new covenant people by the Spirit (Acts 2:16-21, 33, 38-39). The salvation of Gentiles apart from Jewish covenantal nomism was confirmed by the baptism of the Spirit (Acts 10:44-48; 11:15-17). The decisive argument set forth by Peter at the Jerusalem Conference in support of the Pauline mission to the Gentiles was that God accepted the Gentiles "by giving the Holy Spirit to them just as he did to us" (Acts 15:8). Who, then, could stand in the way of believing Gentiles entering on equal terms with believing Jews if they were co-heirs of the same Spirit of promise? Both the universality of the mission (cf. Gal 3:14; Eph 1:13-14) and its eschatological character were authenticated by the definitive presence of the Spirit from the outset.[52] Paul's post-Damascus life was dedicated to building the new community of God's Spirit-people who would, by the leading of that same Spirit, declare God's salvation to the nations still in darkness.

---

in D. Bosch, "Mission in Paul: Invitation to Join the Eschatological Community," in *Transforming Mission: Paradigm Shift in Theology of Mission* (Maryknoll: Orbis, 1991), 123-78.

[52]This is developed at length in Fee, *God's Empowering Presence*, 803-26.

PART II

HISTORICAL ISSUES

Among the papers submitted to the EMS were two excellent historical accounts of the ministry of the Holy Spirit and mission dynamics. Both papers were from Pentecostal scholars dealing with mission practice since the last century. One of the papers presented was previously submitted for publication and is available in a forthcoming volume: Grant McClung, "Try to Get People Saved: Revisiting the Paradigm of an Urgent Pentecostal Missiology," in *The Globalization of Pentecostalism*, edited by Murray W. Dempster, Byron D. Klaus, and Douglas P. Peterson (Irvine, CA: Regnum Books International).

The second paper is Gary McGee's work on the dynamics of a "radical strategy" which has been an integral part of the missiology among a wider section of Christian missions. McGee examines the linkage between the expectation of the miraculous and the evangelistic outreach of missions. In dealing with the historical record, McGee reminds us that while Pentecostals held firmly to the necessity for supernatural power, there was also an "expectancy of miraculous interventions" among evangelical missions.

Due in part to the lack of papers submitted by other historians, the editorial committee decided that it would be helpful to include an article from the work of Roland Allen. A chapter from a lesser known work by Allen, *Pentecost and the World: The Revelation of the Holy Spirit in 'The Acts of the Apostles'* (London: Oxford University Press, 1917), is included as chapter 5. Allen, in his unapologetic manner, tackles the issues with a different conclusion than many of the contributors. Based on his examination of the biblical account, Allen reminds us of our dependency upon the Spirit who prepares us for responding to his work, while warning us against focusing on the results of our own actions.

An important aspect of the ongoing dialogue must be a careful review of missions history. Judging from the papers submitted, there is a need for more work from other evangelical perspectives to join the contributions included in this section.

4

THE RADICAL STRATEGY IN MODERN MISSION: THE LINKAGE OF PARANORMAL PHENOMENA WITH EVANGELISM

Gary B. McGee

Modern Christianity has undergone several dramatic shifts, not least of which is the extraordinary attention now placed on the role of the Holy Spirit and "spiritual warfare" in the Christian world mission. This study examines the linkage that Christians have made between paranormal phenomena and evangelism and missions, particularly since the last century. It also traces the emergence and significance of the "radical strategy" in missions, a missiological perspective shared to varying degrees by fundamentalists, evangelicals, Pentecostals, and charismatics.

Doubts and Miracles

Expectation of supernatural phenomena, notably miracles as well as the "*charismata*" (gifts of the Holy Spirit [1 Cor 12:8-10]), continued in sectors of Christianity long after the time of the apostles.[1] As a rule, however, 19th cen-

---

[1]Killian McDonnell and George T. Montague, *Christian Initiation and Baptism in the Holy Spirit* (Collegeville, Minn.: Liturgical Press, 1991); Cecil M. Robeck, Jr., *Prophecy in Carthage: Perpetua, Tertullian, and Cyprian* (Cleveland: Pilgrim Press, 1993); Stanley M. Burgess, *The Holy Spirit: Ancient Christian Traditions* (Peabody, Mass.: Hendrickson Publishers, 1984); idem, *The Holy Spirit: Eastern Christian Traditions* (Peabody, Mass.: Hendrickson Publishers, 1989).

tury Protestant and Catholic missionaries doubted the availability of miracles.[2] Alexander Duff, the renowned Scottish missionary to India, wrote in 1839, "Missionaries of the Church of Scotland have been sent forth . . . in the absence of miracles."[3] This qualification also surfaced at the 1860 international missions conference in Liverpool, England. When comparing modern missionaries to the apostles, the Reverend Frederick Trestrail, secretary of the Baptist Missionary Society, fluttering above the constraints of logic, said triumphantly: "Divest the Apostles of miraculous power . . . and you have the *modern missionary*, a true successor of the Apostles" (Trestrail's emphasis).[4]

In place of supernatural demonstrations of power, missionaries confidently shared the blessings of their "higher" civilization to further the gospel.[5] For most missionaries, the postmillennial calendar with its optimism of Christianizing society nurtured the hope that after a lengthy period of progress, Christ would return. Therefore, mission schools enlightened students with Western learning so they would see the superiority of Christianity and embrace the faith. In this way, conversion and civilizing worked hand in hand to lead them out of heathen darkness. Nevertheless, given the sizable number of missionaries and financial investment by 1906, the number of converts proved meager indeed (only 3.6 million communicants and adherents).[6]

---

[2]For a Catholic perspective noting the general absence of miracles, see Joseph Schmidlin, *Catholic Mission Theology* (Techny, Ill.: Mission Press, S.V.D., 1931), 341-353.

[3]Alexander Duff, *India, and India Missions* (Edinburgh: John Johnstone, Hunter Square, 1839), xiii.

[4]Frederick Trestrail, "On Native Churches," *Conference on Missions Held in 1860 at Liverpool* (London: James Nisbet & Co., 1860), 279.

[5]E.g., Duff, *India, and India Missions*, 25-26.

[6]Harlan P. Beach, *A Geography and Atlas of Protestant*

Apostolic Methods
Faith for God's Provision

Some missions advocates, however, compared the methods of their day with the simplicity of New Testament evangelism. Could a return to "apostolic" practices bring greater success? As early as 1824, the issue sparked controversy at an anniversary conference of the London Missionary Society. There, six years before a charismatic movement would begin in England under his influence, Presbyterian pastor Edward Irving preached that missionaries should ideally follow the model initiated by Jesus in Matthew 10:9-10: "Provide neither gold nor silver, nor brass in your purses. Nor scrip for your journey, neither two coats, neither shoes, nor yet staves: for the workman is worthy of his meat."[7]

Due to the slow pace of conversions overseas, Irving proposed that missionaries depend on faith in God for resources rather than simply on the benevolence of mission agencies. The "nobleness of the missionary character" requires dependence on "the Spirit of God, for sustenance, for patronage, for reward, and for a rule of procedure." While God would still bless missionaries who relied on human means, they would do far better if "brought over from resting upon the visible to rest upon the invisible helps, then . . . the full measure of the Lord's blessing [would be] poured out upon his handiwork."[8] Though sharply criticized, Irving had gained a hearing and his addresses were published as

---

Missions, Vol. II: Statistics and Atlas (New York: Student Volunteer Movement for Foreign Missions, 1906), 19.

[7]All scripture quotations are taken from the Authorized Version.

[8]Edward Irving, *Missionaries After the Apostolical School* (Tientsin: Tientsin Printing Co., 1887), 97, 100.

Missionaries After the Apostolical School (1825), a book later considered so valuable by Timothy Richard, the famed missionary to China, that he reprinted it in 1887 and sent copies to hundreds of missionaries in China, India, and Japan. Richard was hardly alone in his interest in Matthew 10.

Appearances of Pentecostal Phenomena

Many looked to spiritual awakenings to provide the personnel and spiritual empowerment necessary to accomplish the missionary task. For example, when news of the American "Prayer Revival" of 1858 reached Northern Ireland (Ulster), startled Presbyterians noted unusual happenings, especially hundreds of people falling to the ground—"stricken" or "prostrated" by God's power under intense conviction of sin.[9] When word of this reached Tinnevelly (present-day Tamil Nadu) in South India, believers there, strongly influenced by the ecclesiology and dispensational premillennial eschatology of the Plymouth Brethren, spoke in tongues, prophesied, recounted visions, fell prostrate, prayed for the sick, helped the poor, and evangelized non-Christians.[10] Anglican missionary Ashton Dibb (Church Missionary Society) declared the impact to be unprecedented in the history of Indian missions: "It certainly does seem to have at least the merit of being the *first entirely indigenous effort of the native church at self-extension*" (Dibb's emphasis).[11] Another missionary, noting the precedent of

---

[9]Many such accounts appear in William Reid, *Authentic Records of Revival, Now in Progress in the United Kingdom* (London: James Nisbet & Co., 1860).

[10]For details of the revival, see G. H. Lang, ed., *The History and Diaries of an Indian Christian* (London: Thynne & Co., 1939).

[11]Ashton Dibb, "The Revival in North Tinnevelly," *Church Missionary Record*, V, New Series (August 1860): 178.

Matthew 10, reported, "It is indeed a new era in Indian Missions—that of lay converts going forth without purse or scrip to preach the Gospel of Christ to their fellow-countrymen (sic), and that with a zeal and life we had hardly thought them capable of."[12]

In another part of the world, missionary Johannes Warneck recorded that from the 1860s the Indonesian Christian community increased after the appearance of similar "Pentecostal" phenomena: dreams, visions, signs in the heavens, and several instances where missionaries (e.g., Ludwig Nommensen) unwittingly drank poison given by their enemies and remained unharmed (Joel 2:28-29; Mark 16:18).[13] Convinced they had "fulfilled their purpose of pointing the stupefied heathen to the gift of the Gospel," Warneck saw "the power of working signs and wonders" (Acts 5:12) as simply temporary, just as they had been in early Christianity.[14]

Yet, Theodore Christlieb, a well-known German theologian and premillennialist, took a different view. Aware of the happenings in Indonesia, he contended that "in the last epoch of the consummation of the Church . . . she will again require for her final decisive struggle with the powers of darkness, the miraculous interference of her risen Lord, and hence the Scriptures lead us to expect miracles once more for this period." Christlieb then noted that "in the history of modern missions we find many wonderful occurrences which unmistakably remind us of the apostolic age."[15]

---

[12]Ibid., 185.

[13]Joh. Warneck, *The Living Christ and Dying Heathenism*, 3rd ed. (New York: Fleming H. Revell Co., n.d.), 175-182; Theodore Christlieb, *Modern Doubt and Christian Belief* (New York: Scribner, Armstrong & Co., 1874), 334.

[14]Ibid., 182, 165.

[15]Christlieb, *Modern Doubt*, 332.

Expectancy of supernatural interventions in missions during the "last days" also characterized the labors of Seventh-Day Adventist missionaries in the 19th and early 20th centuries, believers historically excluded from the ranks of mainstream Christians. Nonetheless, stories of gospel proclamation and miracles in the history of their missions—the accounts of "special providence"—clearly parallel those of radical evangelicals.[16]

Divine Intervention

Believers who contended that supernatural "signs" should accompany the preaching of the gospel not only appealed to Matthew 10, but increasingly to Mark 16:17-18, though cognizant of the textual problem with the passage.[17] This interest set the stage for the "radical strategy"—an apocalyptic scenario of divine intervention in signs and wonders to ensure that every tribe and nation would hear the gospel before the close of human history (Matt 24:14; Acts 1:8).[18] Those who reflected on the availability of miracles included, among others, Christlieb; Anthony Norris

---

[16]See William A. Spicer, *Miracles of Modern Missions* (Washington, D.C.: Review and Herald Publishing Association, 1926).

[17]E.g., A. J. Gordon, *The Ministry of Healing* (Harrisburg, PA: Christian Publications, n.d.; originally published in 1882), 245-246.

[18]For contemporary criticisms of the radical strategy, see "A New Missionary Movement," *The Gospel in All Lands*, February 9, 1882, 61-62 (the author decries "these flying squadrons of extemporised Missionaries"); Charles C. Tracy, "False Notions About the Evangelization of the World," *The Gospel in All Lands*, June 1891, 269-270; Ashbel Green, *Presbyterian Missions* (New York: Anson D. F. Randolph & Co., 1893), 138-139; Green condemns "exceptional theories."

Groves (Plymouth [Open] Brethren missionary to India); Thomas Erskine (Scottish lay theologian); Edward Irving; and Horace Bushnell (an American theologian).[19] This list, however, would be incomplete without the name of George Muller, a well-known philanthropist whose expectant faith for God's provision at his orphan homes in Bristol, England, modeled the idealized "faith life" for many Christians and inspired the growing number of independent "faith" missionaries. Although not remembered for advocacy of signs and wonders, his perspectives on faith and the remarkable answers to his prayers helped lay the theoretical basis.[20]

A wide spectrum of Protestants, both at home and on the mission fields, prayed throughout the century for the outpouring of the Spirit as predicted by the prophet Joel (2:28-32).[21] Many hoped that spiritual awakenings would lead to effective evangelism and reforming society of its evils (e.g., slavery, drunkenness, political corruption).[22] At the

---

[19]G. H. Lang, *Anthony Norris Groves* (London: Thynne & Co., 1939); C. Gordon Strachan, *The Pentecostal Theology of Edward Irving* (London: Darton, Longman & Todd, 1973); Thomas Erskine, *The Supernatural Gifts of the Spirit*, ed. R. Kelso Carter (Philadelphia: Office of "Words of Faith," 1883); Horace Bushnell, *Nature and The Supernatural* (New York: Charles Scribner, 1858), 446-528.

[20]See Arthur T. Pierson, *George Muller of Bristol* (New York: Baker and Taylor Co., 1899).

[21]Significantly, A. J. Gordon emphasized Spirit baptism, an empowerment of the believer subsequent to conversion, in his keynote address to the first international convention of the Student Volunteer Movement; see "The Holy Spirit and Missions," *Student Mission Power: Report of the First International Convention of the Student Volunteer Movement for Foreign Missions Held at Cleveland, Ohio, U.S.A., February 26, 27, 28 and March 1, 1891*, 7-20.

[22]Timothy L. Smith, *Revivalism and Social Concern: American Protestantism on the Eve of the Civil War* (New York:

same time, and due to the slow advance of medical science and the cries of the terminally ill, some Christians (usually those with ties to the holiness movement) examined scriptural promises of healing (e.g., Isa 53:4-5; James 5:13-16).[23] The emphasis on healing subsequently opened the door wider to miracles since all of the charismatic gifts might too be restored (1 Cor 12:10).

Finally, after the American Civil War a small but growing cadre of premillennialists began to negatively assess human advancement. On their chart, the world would go from bad to worse before Christ's return. With the end of the century nearing, an arms race heating up between the major powers, increasing political and military tensions ("wars and rumors of wars"), and Zionists calling for a Jewish homeland in Palestine, many speculated that Christ would return by 1900 or thereabouts. With deepening concern, keen observers of the missions scene wondered how the great commission could be accomplished in such a short time.

The Radical Strategy
Faith for Miracles

More than others after mid-century, A. B. Simpson, the former Presbyterian minister who founded the Christian and Missionary Alliance (CMA), and A. J. Gordon, chairman of the executive committee of the American Baptist Missionary Union, put theory into action by encouraging the

---

Harper & Row, Publishers, 1957), 114-162.

[23]Leonard I. Sweet, *Health and Medicine in the Evangelical Tradition* (Valley Forge, PA: Trinity Press International, 1994), 135-161; cf., Paul Gale Chappell, "The Diving Healing Movement in America," Ph.D. dissertation, Drew University, 1983.

faithful to trust God for miracles, especially physical healings. Both started Bible institutes, along with Dwight L. Moody, to train men and women for ministry at home and abroad: the Missionary Training Institute (1882), Boston Missionary Training School (1886), and Chicago Evangelization Society (1889), respectively. Because they departed from conventional college and seminary curricula, critics claimed that the "short-cut" offered by these schools produced poorly trained candidates for ministry.

Gordon contended that "the rigid logic which is supposed to fence out miracles from modern christendom, does not seem to have been careful to include heathendom in its prohibition. For when it is said that 'miracles belong to the planting of Christianity not to its progress and development,' it will at once strike us that missions are practically the planting of Christianity."[24] In his estimation, neither the gifts of tongues and prophecy nor the occurrence of miracles were "confined within the first age of the church."[25]

Other radical evangelicals shared this optimism about the potential advantages of the Spirit's empowerment in the praxis of missions. Seeking a special baptism of power, the celebrated "Cambridge Seven" of athletic fame in England arrived in China in 1885 to serve as missionaries with the China Inland Mission. While journeying up the Han River, three of them, C. T. Studd, Cecil Polhill-Turner, and Arthur Polhill-Turner, put their Chinese grammar books aside and prayed for the Pentecostal bestowment of the Chinese language and supernatural power according to the promise of Mark 16:17-18 ("they shall speak with new tongues"). Criticized as "idle fanatics," Studd reported that they finally returned to their books.[26]

---

[24]Gordon, *Ministry of Healing*, 116.

[25]Ibid., 55.

[26]C. T. Studd, "Trumpet Calls to Britain's Sons," in *The Evangelisation of the World, A Missionary Band: A Record of*

Others shared this expectancy which sometimes led to unusual accounts of spiritual gifts. In South India in 1881, Miss C. M. Reade of the Highways and Hedges Mission (Plymouth [Open] Brethren in theology) prayed to receive the gift of speaking Hindustani to communicate directly to her hearers. As a result, "'the power came to her as a gift from God.' One month she was unable to do more than put two or three sentences together; while the next month, she was able to preach and pray without waiting for a word. Those who heard her could only say with herself, 'It was a gift from above.'"[27] Eight years later, China missionary Jona-

----

Consecration, and an Appeal, 3rd ed., ed. B. Broomhall (London: Morgan & Scott, 1889), 53; A. J. Broomhall, Hudson Taylor & China's Open Century, Book Six (London: Hodder & Stoughton, 1988), 375-376; cf., Alvyn Austin, "Missions Dream Team," Christian History, 52 (Vol. XV, 4), 20-21. Two of the Cambridge Seven later had links to the Pentecostal movement. Stanley Smith endorsed the ministry of the American holiness-Pentecostal evangelist Maria B. Woodworth-Etter, as well as the fledgling Pentecostal movement, in "An Appreciation: A Word from a Well-Known Missionary," in M. B. Woodworth-Etter, Signs and Wonders, 6th ed. (Indianapolis, Ind.: By the author, 1916), v. Another member, Cecil H. Polhill-Turner, joined the movement and with A. A. Boddy founded the Pentecostal Missionary Union for Great Britain and Ireland in 1909 modeled after the China Inland Mission; see Peter Hocken, "Cecil H. Polhill—Pentecostal Layman," Pneuma: The Journal of the Society for Pentecostal Studies 10 (Fall 1988): 116-140.

[27]"A Gift of Tongues," New Zealand Christian Record, April 14, 1881, 11; for more information on Reade and the mission she directed, see Miss C. M. Reade, "Punruti Mission," Missionary Conference: South India and Ceylon, 1879 (Madras: Addison & Co., 1880), 2:421-422. William Taylor, Methodist bishop for Africa, referred to a similar account of a young woman missionary under his charge in Africa; see W. B. Godbey, Spiritual Gifts and Graces (Cincinnati: God's Revivalist Office, 1895), 42-43.

than Goforth, a Canadian Presbyterian and premillennialist, claimed that he gained mastery of Mandarin only after receiving supernatural enablement on one occasion.[28] In 1892, an Anglican missionary in Japan, W. P. Buncombe, reported that although he could not "speak fluently at all on any other subjects," yet, "when preaching the Gospel the Holy Ghost makes me forget that I know but little Japanese, and I find, too, that the listeners understand."[29]

Meanwhile, opponents scorned the anticipation of miracles as absurd and irresponsible. A hot debate erupted when E. F. Baldwin, a Southern Baptist and independent missionary to North Africa, contended that Jesus had established Matthew 10 as the divinely ordained pattern for missionaries to follow and that the gospel should be accompanied by supernatural signs. Skeptical of his proposal, Fanny E. Guinness, editor of the *Regions Beyond* (Regions Beyond Missionary Union [U.K.]), sniffed that for the heathen, "miracles cannot enlighten their dark minds, or soften their hard hearts . . . . Our aim is to enlighten, not to astonish."[30] Like many others, she didn't foresee the impact that healings and "power encounters" (e.g., exorcisms, etc.) would have in capturing the attention of non-Christians in Third World countries.

---

[28]Rosalind Goforth, *Goforth of China* (Minneapolis: Bethany Fellowship, n.d.; originally published in 1937), 87-88.

[29]"Japan Mission," *Proceedings of the Church Missionary Society for Africa and the East, 1891-1892*, 209.

[30]Mrs. H. Grattan Guinness, "Missionaries According to Matt. X. A Critique," *Regions Beyond* (April 1889): 110; idem, "Missionaries According to Matt. X. The Questions of Modern Miracles," *Regions Beyond* (November 1889): 358-371.

Divinely Bestowed Languages

Along with other radical evangelicals influenced by dispensational premillennialism, A. B. Simpson announced: "We are preaching the gospel not for the conversion of the world, but for a witness unto all nations, and when we shall have accomplished this, [Christ] will come."[31] Thus, the message had to get out regardless of the number converted. The obstacle of formal language study, however, prevented missionaries from immediately evangelizing once they had arrived on their mission fields. While believing that God would heal the sick as the gospel was proclaimed, he also considered it possible that the Spirit might confer known languages (i.e., speaking in tongues) to eliminate the need for language school and expedite preaching to every tribe and nation (Matt 24:14). He noted that "instances are not wanting now of its apparent restoration in missionary labours both in India and Africa."[32] Hence, "the plan of the Lord [is] to pour out His Spirit not only in the ordinary, but also in the extraordinary gifts and operations of His power . . . as His people press forward to claim the evangelization of the entire world."[33] Consequently, "a mighty baptism of

---

[31]A. B. Simpson, "The New Testament Standpoint of Missions," *Christian Alliance and Missionary Weekly*, December 16, 1892, 390.

[32]Simpson's statement is cited in Mrs. [Fanny] H. Grattan Guinness, "Faith-Healing and Missions," *Regions Beyond*, January 1891, 31; see also, A. B. Simpson, "The Gift of Tongues," *Christian Alliance and Missionary Weekly*, February 12, 1892, 98-99.

[33]A. B. Simpson, "Connection Between Supernatural Gifts and the World's Evangelization," *Christian Alliance and Missionary Weekly*, October 7 & 14, 1892, 226.

the Holy Ghost on all the machinery on the mission field could bring the world's evangelization in a few years."[34]

Nevertheless, the actual application of the radical strategy brought mixed results. John Condit, one of the first Alliance missionaries to the Belgian Congo (present-day Zaire), died from a fever in 1885 shortly after his arrival.[35] Yet Grace Agar, an Alliance missionary to China and Tibet, realizing that medical assistance would be difficult to find, trusted Christ as her healer. She later wrote that the Lord had kept her in strength and health for thirty-eight years and "protected [her] from all harm, from accidents on ice, slippery roads, from robbers, wild beasts and from epidemics so common in China."[36]

In a widely known attempt in 1890, missionaries from the Topeka, Kansas, Y.M.C.A. (the "Kansas-Soudan movement"), allegedly influenced by Simpson, arrived in Sierra Leone confident of biblical promises of healing and Pentecostal tongues.[37] After discovering their need to learn the native dialect, they persevered, but three died from malaria, having refused to take quinine.[38] Holding Simpson re-

---

[34]Simpson, "New Testament Standpoint," 389. Nineteenth century fascination with inventions and the speed and efficiency of "machinery" accounts for the use of this metaphor in the missionary literature.

[35]G. P. Pardington, *Twenty-five Wonderful Years, 1889-1914* (New York: Christian Alliance Publishing Co., 1914), 129, 193-194.

[36]Grace C. Agar, "Tibetan Border of Kansu Province," 14. (Typewritten.) Available at the Assemblies of God Archives, Springfield, Mo. 65802.

[37]The Kansas missionaries' expectation of Pentecostal tongues caught the attention of the noted Anglican linguist, Robert Needham Cust in his *Evangelization of the Non-Christian World* (London: Luzac & Co., 1894), 106-107.

[38]Arthur T. Pierson, "Editorial Notes on Current Topics,"

sponsible for their adoption of his "unscriptural and reason-revolting doctrine," Guinness told her readers that "he thinks too, like Irving before him, that we may expect, and are even beginning to see, a restoration of the gift of tongues."[39]

Despite these tragic failures, the ideal still challenged believers to expect God to bestow linguistic proficiencies. In 1892, Alliance missionaries William W. Simpson and William Christie arrived in China intent on evangelizing Tibet, then considered by some to be the "uttermost part of the earth" (Acts 1:8). Like C. T. Studd and the Polhill-Turner brothers, they anticipated receiving the necessary languages (Mandarin and Tibetan) as gifts from God in fulfillment of Mark 16:17.[40] With the Lord's return imminent, little time remained for the nuisance of language study; expectant faith, however, could achieve the impossible. Responding to

---

Missionary Review of the World, III (New Series) (November 1890): 867-869; C. Howard Hopkins, "The Kansas-Sudan Missionary Movement in the Y.M.C.A., 1889-1891," *Church History* XXI (December 1952): 314-322. Hopkins discusses the controversy over a mission agency within the Y.M.C.A., but says little about events in Sierra Leone. However, awareness of the endeavor with the missionaries' anticipation of tongues and healing, and the subsequent deaths of several, became widely known in mission circles. As late as 1943, Samuel M. Zwemer referred to the story while warning potential missionaries about presumption in his *Into All The World: The Great Commission* (Grand Rapids: Zondervan Publishing House, 1943), 179.

[39]Guinness, "Faith-Healing," 28, 31.

[40]William W. Simpson, "Letter from Shanghai, China," *Christian Alliance and Missionary Weekly,* July 1, 1892, 13-14; A. B. Simpson, "Supernatural Aid in the Study of Foreign Languages," *Christian Alliance and Missionary Weekly,* October 21, 1892, 259-260; idem, "The Supernatural Gifts and Ministries of the Church," *Christian Alliance and Foreign Missionary Weekly,* January 19, 1898, 53-54, 67.

the flurry of interest in missionary tongues, but wishing to avoid the "dangers of Irvingism," the Alliance convention in October 1892 issued an urgent call for the faithful to pray for "the special outpouring of the Spirit in connection with the acquiring of foreign languages and the resistance of the climatic difficulties of Africa, India, and China. We are sure that God has it in His heart to specially signalize His promise in this connection."[41] Interest in missionary tongues continued into the 20th century.

End-Times Missionaries

Clearly the radical strategy emerged from those few like Gordon, Baldwin, Simpson, the Kansas missionaries, and others who believed that God would provide supernatural assistance. One radical, Frank W. Sandford, who had connections to the Alliance, founded the Holy Ghost and Us Bible School at Shiloh, Maine, to prepare an elite band of end-times missionaries, and organized "The World's Evangelization Crusade on Apostolic Principles."[42] In accentuating the cosmic dimension of spiritual warfare in confronting the powers of darkness on mission fields, he later purchased a schooner and barkentine and led his followers on cruises around the world, praying as they passed the coast of each country that God would release His power for its conversion.[43]

Among others, Arthur E. Street, a Presbyterian missionary to Hainan, China, believed that prayerful intercession could bind the "strongman" (the evil spirit ruling over

---

[41]Simpson, "Connection," 226-227.

[42]Frank W. Sandford, *Seven Years with God* (Mount Vernon, N.H.: The Kingdom Press, 1957), 111-132.

[43]Frank S. Murray, *The Sublimity of Faith: The Life and Work of Frank W. Sandford* (Amherst, N.H.: Kingdom Press, 1981), 406-461.

each country, such as the "prince of China") and offered the key to successful evangelism (Matt 12:29); other missionaries shared this perspective as well.[44] Nearly a century later, Third Wave mission leaders proposed a somewhat similar approach to bringing the nations under the dominion of God through binding the "territorial spirits."[45]

In the Midwest, Walter S. and Frances Black and Jennie Glassey testified to Spirit baptism and receiving new languages during an 1895 revival in St. Louis, Missouri. Walter Black, a Canadian Baptist minister, first met Glassey in 1894 while preaching in a rural area of the state. A year after receiving a vision in which she was called to Africa and promised an African language (March 23, 1894), Glassey received a "wonderful language lesson" on July 8-9, 1895, speaking in several African dialects: "Housa," "Croo," "Khoominar," and later the "Chinese language."[46] The Blacks too received languages, but through the "laying on of hands" by members of their church in St. Louis and claiming the promise of Mark 16:17. George B. Peck, M.D., a prominent leader in the Christian and Missionary Alliance living in Boston, endorsed the veracity of these accounts.[47]

Before long, they too headed for Sierra Leone led by "signs, wonders, miracles, healings, tongues and proph-

---

[44]E.g., Alfred E. Street, *Intercessory Foreign Missionaries: Practical Suggestions From a Missionary To Earnest Christians* (Boston: American Advent Mission Society, c.1903-c.1923), 5-11; Moody Press (Chicago, IL) later reprinted the pamphlet under the title *How to Pray for Missionaries* [n.d.]).

[45]C. Peter Wagner, "Territorial Spirits and World Missions," *Evangelical Missions Quarterly* 25 (July 1989): 278-288.

[46]"Mission Work," *Amherst (N.S.) Daily News*, December 9, 1895.

[47]"Tongues of Fire," "Other Tongues," *Tongues of Fire*, April 15, 1896, 58.

ecy."[48] On their way in 1897, they stayed in Liverpool where Glassey spoke to an old sailor acquainted with the Khoominar language. Upon hearing her speak in the dialect, "the power of God settled upon him, and then and there he broke down, confessed his sins, and became a Christian."[49] In view of this, Black remarked, "The same power that drove the arrow of conviction into the hardened heart of an old sailor as he listened to a young girl speaking a language she had never heard in the power of the Holy Ghost, that same power will convict unconverted people, even as it did on the day of Pentecost." In view of their new-found abilities, he looked at contemporary mission endeavors and crowed that neither "20,000 nor 100,000 missionaries of the common sanctified type will [ever] evangelize this globe." Instead, God's church should operate "with purely Holy Ghost machinery," implying that when believers received Spirit baptism, they would speak with new languages. In looking to the future, he predicted that "God Almighty is raising up such a movement, and the last mighty billow that is to sweep over this globe and prepare the way for the coming of the Son of Man, is the movement that will 'Tarry

---

[48]"Commit Thy Way," *Tongues of Fire*, June 15, 1898, 93. It was in Liverpool that the Blacks and Glassey met Frank W. Sandford for the first time. Sandford then gave them passage on his ship to Jerusalem; their reasons for going to Palestine instead of Sierra Leone and immediate whereabouts after that are presently unknown. Charles F. Parham reported in 1902 that "after being a missionary in Africa [Glassey] became a resident of Jerusalem;" see his *Voice Crying in the Wilderness*, 2nd ed. (Baxter Springs, Kan.: Apostolic Faith Bible College, n.d.; originally published in 1902; 2nd ed., 1910), 29. In 1904, Walter Black began pastoring Baptist churches once again. See Murray, *Sublimity of Faith*, 180-191.

[49]"Tarry Until," *Tongues of Fire*, March 1, 1897, 38.

Until.'"[50] Clearly, the contours of Pentecostals' later adaptation of the radical strategy had already begun to take shape as early as the 1880s and '90s.

A Midwestern holiness preacher, Charles F. Parham, took special interest in Sandford's teachings as well as the missionary implications of Glassey's testimony, printing her account in his own *Apostolic Faith* (Topeka, Kan.) newspaper in 1899.[51] In April 1900, he announced that a "Bro. and Sister Hamaker" resided at his headquarters in Topeka, Kansas, "to labor for Jesus until He gives them an heathen tongue, and then they will proceed to the missionary field."[52] During the summer, Parham visited A. B. Simpson's Missionary Training Institute at Nyack, New York, and then Shiloh, Maine, where he heard speaking in tongues for the first time. Convinced that the gift of tongues represented crucial evidence of Spirit baptism and offered the key to unlocking ministry in signs and wonders, Parham and his students at Bethel Bible School in Topeka prayed in January 1901 for the fulfillment of Joel's prophecy. This would then form them as God's special band of divinely empowered missionaries.

Participants testified, as others did at the later Azusa Street Revival (1906-1909) in Los Angeles, California, and elsewhere, that God had given them the languages of the world.[53] Referring to Matthew 10:8-10 and Mark 16:17, one report from Los Angeles boasted, "God is solving the missionary problem, sending out new-tongued mission-

---

[50]Ibid. A reference to Luke 24:49.

[51]"The Gift of Tongues," *Apostolic Faith*, May 3, 1899, 5.

[52]Untitled news note, *Apostolic Faith* (Topeka, Kan.), April 1, 1900, 7, col. 2.

[53]"A Queer Faith," *Topeka Daily Capital, January 6, 1901*, 2; also, James R. Goff, Jr., *Fields White Unto Harvest: Charles F. Parham and the Missionary Origins of Pentecostalism* (Fayetteville, Ark.: University of Arkansas Press, 1988), 62-86.

aries on the apostolic faith line, without purse or scrip, and the Lord is going before them preparing the way."[54] Missionaries could now bypass language school and leave immediately for the mission fields to begin preaching the gospel.[55]

Radical Beyond Reason?

The language proposal severely tested the credulity of their fellow evangelicals, but retained an empirical tinge––languages could be verified. Yet evidence that Pentecostals did in fact preach in new languages proved difficult to find. By late 1906 and 1907, though still believing that tongues signified human languages or those of angels (1 Cor 13:1), Pentecostals began to view tongues speech as "glossolalia" (i.e., unknown tongues to speaker and hearer), bringing empowerment through worship and intercession in the Spirit (1 Cor 14:2).[56] In turn, glossolalia and the recovery of all the gifts of the Spirit generated a restorationist dynamic in spirituality that has had a marked influence on modern Christianity.

Notwithstanding, critics branded speaking in tongues as nonsense. What's more, Pentecostals had "crossed the Rubicon" into irrational behavior and stumbled into the satanic realm.[57] Scrutinizing the rapid expansion of

---

[54]Untitled note, *Apostolic Faith* (Los Angeles), November 1906, 2, col. 4.

[55]"Parham's New Religion Practiced at 'Stone's Folly,'" *Kansas City Times*, January 27, 1901, 55.

[56]E.g., A. G. Garr, "Tongues, the Bible Evidence," *A Cloud of Witnesses to Pentecost in India*, September 1907, 42-44; A. A. Boddy, "Speaking in Tongues: What is It?" *Confidence*, May 1910, 100.

[57]E.g., G. H. Lang, *The Modern Gift of Tongues: Whence Is It?* (London: Marshall Brothers, 1913), 115-132. Ironically, Lang

Pentecostalism, the fiery holiness bishop Alma White fumed that the "old Red Dragon" had caused it to spread so quickly around the world.[58] Speaking in tongues might sound to some like a real language, but those who engaged in it had already been "caught in the devil's delusive net," even though liking to "talk about the blood of the atonement, claim to heal diseases, and especially take up the theme of the second coming of Christ."[59]

Evangelical Christians were already becoming aware of the encroachment of Christian Science, Theosophy, and Spiritualism, the latter two enmeshed in occult practices.[60] Kenneth Mackenzie, a leader in the Christian and Missionary Alliance, warned believers in his *Anti-Christian Supernaturalism* (1901) that "God's work of grace is ever paralleled by another force energising (sic) a contrary spirit."[61] To make matters worse, not only did speaking in tongues appear among spiritualists, but Mormons as well.[62] If these threats failed to rattle the serenity of the faithful, Presbyte-

---

accepted as scripturally valid the speaking in tongues that occurred among Brethren believers in South India in 1860-1865, but rejected the phenomena that occurred in the early Pentecostal movement; see his *History and Diaries*.

[58]Alma White, *Demons and Tongues* (Zarephath, N.J.: Pillar of Fire, 1936), 99.

[59]Ibid., 16.

[60]Evangelical advocates of faith healing faced accusations of "mind control," Spiritualism, and Christian Science; for a defense of the doctrine, see Glen Wood, "What Divine Healing Is Not," *Christian Alliance*, January 1888, 7.

[61]Kenneth Mackenzie, Jr., *Anti-Christian Supernaturalism* (New York: New York: Christian Alliance Publishing Co., 1901), 11.

[62]See John L. Brooke, *The Refiner's Fire: The Making of Mormon Cosmology, 1644-1844* (New York: Cambridge University Press, 1994.)

rian missionary John L. Nevius did by telling of exorcisms in China where demons had spoken in tongues.[63]

Expecting Miracles

To empower the faithful for evangelism, most Pentecostals taught that every Christian should seek for Spirit baptism as initially evidenced by speaking in tongues, and pray to receive the gifts of the Spirit.[64] In evangelizing, they prioritized the need for spectacular displays of celestial power—signs and wonders, healing, and deliverance from sinful habits and satanic bondage, but spent little time wrestling with the issue of the sovereignty of God and why more people were not healed.[65]

Pentecostals quickly became adept at planning, but insisted that "well-oiled" campaign techniques could never substitute for demonstrations of supernatural power. Emphasis on the importance of miracles has born fruit in many countries. In Buenos Aires, Argentina in 1954, a spectacular evangelistic campaign led by evangelist Tommy Hicks and sponsored by Pentecostal and evangelical churches changed the religious landscape. With an aggregate attendance of nearly two million people, and driven by testimonies of notable healings and deliverances, the meetings resulted in a

---

[63]John L. Nevius, *Demon Possession and Allied Themes* (New York: Fleming H. Revell Co., 1896), 46-47, 58-59.

[64]For perspectives on the classical Pentecostal view of Spirit baptism, see Gary B. McGee, ed., *Initial Evidence: Historical and Biblical Perspectives on the Pentecostal Doctrine of Spirit Baptism* (Peabody, MA: Hendrickson Publishers, 1991).

[65]A notable exception was the British Assemblies of God leader Donald Gee and his controversial *Trophimus I Left Sick: Our Problems of Divine Healing* (London: Elim Publishing Co., 1952).

major breakthrough for Protestantism.[66] Thirty years later an even greater awakening, characterized again by signs and wonders, garnered international attention.[67]

Expectancy of miraculous interventions continued in the ranks of evangelicals, but with more caution and less fanfare than Pentecostals accorded them. Cessationism, controversy over the "tongues movement" and faith healing, and fears of subjective religious experience produced hesitations that until recently have generally kept fundamentalists and evangelicals from seeking signs and wonders.[68] Nevertheless, healings, exorcisms, and other extraordinary events have occurred in the ministries of missionaries in the Christian and Missionary Alliance, National Holiness Missionary Society (later World Gospel Mission), Church of the Nazarene, Missionary Church Association, China Inland Mission (later Overseas Missionary Fellowship), Presbyterian Church (U.S.A.), Southern Baptist Convention, Unevangelized Field Mission, and Worldwide Evangelization Crusade, among others.[69]

---

[66]Arno W. Enns, *Man, Milieu and Mission in Argentina* (Grand Rapids: William B. Eerdmans Publishing Co., 1971), 76-78; Louie W. Stokes, *The Great Revival in Buenos Aires* (Buenos Aires: Casilla De Correo, 1954).

[67]C. Peter Wagner, *The Third Wave of the Holy Spirit* (Ann Arbor, MI: Vine Books, 1988), 93-100. For a recent classical Pentecostal exposition on the role of the supernatural in evangelism, see Benny C. Aker and Gary B. McGee, eds., *Signs and Wonders in Ministry Today* (Springfield, MO: Gospel Publishing House, 1996).

[68]For the debate on the cessation of miracles and the charismata at the end of the apostolic period, see Benjamin B. Warfield, *Counterfeit Miracles* (London: Banner of Truth Trust, 1972; originally published 1918); cf. Jon Ruthven, *On the Cessation of the Charismata: The Protestant Polemic on Postbiblical Miracles* (Sheffield, U.K.: Sheffield Academic Press, 1993).

[69]E.g., Charles W. Nienkirchen, *A. B. Simpson and the*

Cecil Troxel, a missionary to China with the National Holiness Missionary Society, participated in many exorcisms during his more than forty years of overseas service (1901-1943) and observed that "many Chinese who became Christians were first convinced that Jesus is divine because they witnessed His power to cast out demons."[70] In 1932, Southern Baptist missionaries in Shantung Province, North China, reported numerous miraculous happenings during a time of revival, including that of a young bandit who had been struck blind and his face became swollen. Seeing this as a judgment from God for his sins, he repented

---

Pentecostal Movement (Peabody, Mass.: Hendrickson Publishers, 1992), 122-128; R. A. Jaffray, "'Speaking in Tongues'—Some Words of Kindly Counsel," *Alliance Weekly*, March 13, 1909, 395, 396, 406; W. W. Cary, *Story of the National Holiness Missionary Society*, 2d ed. (Chicago: National Holiness Missionary Society, 1941), 48, 189; Russell V. DeLong and Mendell Taylor, *Fifty Years of Nazarene Missions*, Vol. II: *History of the Fields* (Kansas City, MO: Beacon Hill Press, 1955), 291-292, 294; J. A. Ringenberg, *Jesus the Healer* (Fort Wayne, IN: Missionary Church Association, 1947), 76; Dr. and Mrs. Howard Taylor, *Hudson Taylor and the China Inland Mission: The Growth of a Work of God* (Philadelphia: China Inland Mission, 1918), 529; Jonathan and Rosalind Goforth, *Miracle Lives of China*, ed. Mary Goforth Moynan (Elkhart, IN: Bethel Publishing, 1988); Mary K. Crawford, *The Shantung Revival* [Southern Baptist] (Decatur, TX: Rare Christian Books, reprint of original 1933 edition); *This Is That* [Worldwide Evangelization Crusade] (London: Christian Literature Crusade, 1954) [for occurrences of xenolalic tongues, see page 49]; Shirley Horne, *An Hour to the Stone Age* [Unevangelized Fields Mission] (Chicago: Moody Press, 1973).

[70]Cecil Troxel quoted in Mrs. Cecil Troxel and Mrs. John J. Trachsel, *Cecil Troxel: The Man and the Work* (Chicago: National Holiness Missionary Society, 1948), 87.

and was converted, after which he regained his eyesight and the swelling left.[71]

Anticipation of miracles has also been found across an even broader spectrum of evangelical Christians from fundamentalists to members of the historic churches. In 1922, after ten years of praying for the sick, Herbert Pakenham-Walsh, Anglican Bishop of Assam, noted its preeminent importance in mission work and concluded that "God is leading us back at this time to the rediscovery of an almost forgotten truth, and the recapture of a great and wonderful power."[72] Other missionaries participated in power encounters and exorcisms.[73]

Controversy has naturally followed radical evangelicals as they have reformulated the radical strategy. Currently, debate swirls over claims that another missiological paradigm shift has begun, one noted for "strategic-level spiritual warfare" and "spiritual mapping."[74] Shying away from identification with classical Pentecostals and charismatics, leaders such as Charles H. Kraft, C. Peter Wagner, Timothy M. Warner, and John Wimber have adjusted the strategy yet once more.[75] To a limited extent, their views on

---

[71]Mary K. Crawford, *The Shantung Revival* (Decatur, TX: Rare Christian Books, originally published c.1933), 35.

[72]H. Pakenham-Walsh, "Divine Healing: A Record of Missionary Study and Experience," *International Review of Missions* 11 (1922): 101.

[73]E.g., Hugh W. White (Presbyterian), *Demonism Verified and Analyzed* (1922); *Demon Experiences in Many Lands* (Fundamentalist) (1960); and Willard M. Swartley, ed. (Mennonite), *Essays on Spiritual Bondage and Deliverance* (1988).

[74]C. Peter Wagner, *Confronting the Powers* (Ventura, CA: Regal Books, 1996), 22-31.

[75]See Charles H. Kraft, *Christianity with Power: Your Worldview and Your Experience of the Supernatural* (Ann Arbor,

"spiritual warfare" have exceeded those held by 19th century advocates.[76] Once again, critics have called this "radical beyond reason."

The attention to spiritual gifts and power encounters with evil forces in the spiritual realm has proven to be unusually helpful in evangelizing peoples with non-Western worldviews. At the same time, it has contributed to the gradual "Pentecostalization" of much of Third World Christianity in worship and ministry. It continues with great fervor in many regions, from the activities of charismatic Lutherans in Ethiopia, to Catholic evangelizers in Angola and the Philippines (prompted by Vatican II and the charismatic renewal), to the global missionary witness of Singaporean Christians, and the growth of Pentecostal and charismatic movements in Latin America.[77]

MI: Vine Books, 1989); C. Peter Wagner and F. D. Pennoyer, eds., *Wrestling with Dark Angels* (Ventura, CA: Regal Books, 1990); Timothy M. Warner, *Spiritual Warfare: Victory over the Powers of This Dark World* (Wheaton, IL: Crossway Books, 1991); John Wimber and Kevin Springer, *Power Evangelism*, 2d ed. (San Francisco: HarperSanFrancisco, 1992); also, Thomas H. McAlpine, *Facing the Powers: What are the options?* (Monrovia, CA: MARC, 1991).

[76]Ibid., 9-87.

[77]Larry Christenson, ed., *Welcome, Holy Spirit: A Study of Charismatic Renewal in the Church* (Minneapolis: Augsburg Publishing House, 1987), 369-370; Tom Forrest, "Evangelization 2000: A Global View," in *The New Catholic Evangelization*, ed. Kenneth Boyack (New York: Paulist Press, 1992), 214-227; Edward L. Cleary and Hannah W. Steward-Gambino, eds., *Power, Politics, and Pentecostals in Latin America* (Boulder, CO: Westview Press, 1996); Harvey Cox, *Fire from Heaven: The Rise of Pentecostal Spirituality and the Reshaping of Religion in the Twenty-first Century* (Reading, MA: Addison-Wesley Co., 1995).

Conclusion

The quandary over how to bring closure to the Great Commission pressed radical evangelicals in the 19th century to daringly seek the restoration of the Spirit's power as taught and illustrated in the New Testament. From this emerged a blueprint for endtimes evangelism—the radical strategy, a uniquely pneumatological approach to mission adapted in various ways to the present time. For some this has meant praying for physical healings and\or power to exorcise demons; while others added the possibility of receiving known human languages for missionary preaching, thus giving rise to the Pentecostal movement; and still others have sought to "bind the strong man" (Satan) in the cosmic struggle for the salvation of humankind. Believing that God does frequently and directly intervene in human affairs, the legacy of their efforts has contributed to the remarkable growth of Christianity in the 20th century.

Today, the increasing interest in strategic-level spiritual warfare has raised major questions about the believer's authority over the powers of darkness. This requires that related exegetical, theological, and missiological issues receive careful and irenic scrutiny by both practitioners and scholars. Their dialogue on ministry in the power of the Spirit offers a unique opportunity for evangelical Christians of all persuasions to grow in mutual understanding, work together for the advancement of the kingdom of God, and realize greater unity in the body of Christ.

Always controversial because they question traditional and seemingly less effective means of winning converts, radical evangelicals' interest in the ministry of the Spirit in mission has moved the expectancy of signs and wonders from the periphery of Christian missions to the fore. Despite the differences of opinion that always follow new insights and strategies, it should be celebrated that over the last 200 years, the urgency of missions in the "last days" has challenged churches of almost every persuasion to reflect anew on the operation of "Holy Ghost machinery" in the great harvest field of the Christian world mission.

5

THE SPIRIT THE SOURCE AND TEST OF NEW FORMS OF MISSIONARY ACTIVITY[1]

Roland Allen

In the Acts there is revealed a most curious change in the conduct of the apostles before and after Pentecost. Whether St Luke deliberately desired to call our attention to this change is not clear; but in his narrative the change is very apparent. Before Pentecost the apostles are represented as acting under the influence of an intellectual theory; after Pentecost they are represented as acting under the impulse of the Spirit.

The only event recorded after the Ascension before Pentecost is the appointment of Matthias. This appointment was made, we are told, at the instigation of St Peter, and the speech in which he urged it upon his fellow apostles is reported. St Peter found a passage in the Old Testament which seemed to him to foretell the defection of Judas. This passage ended with the words, "His office let another take." From this St Peter concluded that the apostles ought to choose a man to fill the position left vacant by the death of the traitor. Here there is implied an argument which is yet more clearly expressed in the prayer which follows: "Thou Lord, which knowest the hearts of all men, show of these two the one whom thou hast chosen, to take the place in this ministry and apostleship, from which Judas fell away." The argument is that Christ appointed twelve apostles: that one had fallen away and perished: the number of apostles was

---

[1]This chapter originally appeared in Roland Allen's *Pentecost and the World: The Revelation of the Holy Spirit in 'The Acts of the Apostles.'* London: Oxford University Press, 1917.

therefore incomplete: consequently it was the duty of the apostles to restore it by appointing a new member.

Convinced by this argument, they resolved to appoint one of those who had been with them from the beginning and was a witness of the Resurrection. There were many who satisfied these conditions. In order to determine which of these should be appointed to the vacant office, they first selected two, and then adopted a method commonly practiced in the Old Testament to discover the will of God: they cast lots. The lot fell upon Matthias, and he was numbered with the eleven apostles.

By casting lots the apostles revealed that they had not that clear and intuitive apprehension of the will of God which sometimes marked the actions of some of the Old Testament prophets. When Samuel, for instance, went to Bethlehem, and Jesse made his sons to pass before him, the prophet, as he viewed each one, was perfectly clear that he knew the mind of God. "The Lord hath not chosen this," he said again and again, until it almost appeared that he had rejected the whole family. At last, when David was sent for and brought in, he recognized at once the man whom the Lord had chosen, and anointed him. The apostles had not this certain knowledge: they adopted a method used by those who were in doubt as to the mind of God.

Thus, in the account given by St Luke of the appointment of Matthias, these two points stand out with remarkable clearness: first, that the action of the apostles was based upon an intellectual theory, and secondly that they had no definite spiritual guidance which revealed to them unmistakably any individual disciple as called by Christ to the apostolate.

After Pentecost a very remarkable change is to be seen. The apostles no longer argue: they obey a spiritual impulse. They do not act in obedience to the dictates of an intellectual theory; the one and only guide, both in their own actions and in their judgment of the action of other, is their recognition of the Spirit in themselves and others.

I have already pointed out that St Peter expressed a great understanding of the nature and work of Jesus in his first sermon; but neither he nor his fellow apostles had intellectually grasped the truth which he expressed. They did not begin their work with a reasoned theory. They did not argue that, the nature and work of Christ being universal, they must embrace the whole world in their view. Christ taught this; but the apostles did not grasp it at once. Their view was limited, their understanding partial. But neither did they begin with a theory of the nature and work of Christ, or of the character of their mission which excluded the greater part of the human race, a theory which needed to be revised and corrected as time went on and larger and truer conceptions were admitted. Their view was partial, but it was not false; it was limited, but it was not misleading. So far as they could see, they spoke truly of Christ and of their work; nay, more, they spoke in terms which embraced more than they understood.

This was due to the fact that they did not begin their work under the direction of an intellectual theory, but under the impulse of the Spirit. This Spirit was in its nature worldwide, all-embracing. Consequently they did not gradually enlarge their sympathies, and extend their activities in obedience to the demands of an intellectual progress; the world-embracing spirit enlarged and expanded their sympathy, and intellectual illumination followed. They then perceived the wider and larger application of truths of which they had hitherto seen only the partial application. Study of the doctrine did not lead to the wider activity; enlarged activity led them to understand the doctrine.

Similarly, their sense of the need of men for Jesus Christ was essentially the apprehension of a universal truth. Wherever they might meet men, the men whom they met would share that need which they knew first for themselves and for their fellow countrymen. If they knew the need at all, they knew it for the world. Consequently, when they expressed it, though their thoughts at the moment were turned to a special limited class of men, yet the expression took universal form. They did not argue that the need of this class of men, or of that race of men, was great, and that therefore they must take steps to supply the need. They were moved, not so much by an intellectual apprehension, as by a spiritual illumination. They met men, and the need of those men whom they met cried aloud to them. Their own desire for the revelation of the glory of Jesus in the salvation of men went out towards those whom they met, and was immediately answered by the recognition of the need of those whom they met for Jesus Christ.

Again, Christ had given them a world-wide commission, embracing all the nations; but intellectually they did not understand what He meant. They found that out as they followed the impulse of the Spirit.

They did not base their action upon any intellectual interpretation of the nature and work and command of Christ. Neither did they base their action upon any anticipation of results which might be expected to follow from it. They did not argue that the conversion of any particular class or race of men might be expected greatly to strengthen the Church for her work in the world and therefore they ought to make special efforts to win the adhesion of this class or race. They did not argue that the relaxation or abandonment of familiar rules would inevitably result in serious injury to the Church. They did argue that any particular action of a missionary was to be condemned because, if it were approved, it would seem to undermine some generally accepted doctrine, or would greatly disturb the minds of a large body of Christians, or would lead to developments which might be undesirable. The apostles acted under the impulse of the Spirit; their action was not controlled by the exigencies of any intellectual theory.

This is most manifest in those steps towards the evangelization of the Gentiles upon which St Luke lays special stress. Philip the Evangelist went to meet the Ethiopian under the direct influence of the Spirit, and baptized him without apparently drawing, or expecting others to draw, any conclusions from his action which might involve the whole Church in a policy. In the crucial case of the visit of St Peter to Cornelius, St Peter himself was prepared by a special vision, and evidently realized that his action was liable to be called in question; but he acted under the impulse of the Spirit, though neither he nor the others really understood what consequences were involved in his action. St Peter certainly did not think the matter out, decide that the Gentiles were within the terms of Christ's commission, and then, and therefore, proceed to preach to them. Even St Paul himself did not begin with argument. It was repeatedly revealed to him that he was called to preach to the Gentiles; but only after his action had taken effect, when men disputed and opposed him, did he begin to formulate a theory that results which he saw to be blessed were in truth the fulfillment of Old Testament prophecies and teaching, and a true revelation of the nature and work of Jesus Christ.

Thus the path by which the apostles reached the truth was submissive obedience in act to the impulse of the Holy Spirit. When the moment came, when the Spirit in them moved them to desire men's salvation, and to feel their need, they acted, they spoke, they expressed that Spirit of love and desire, not knowing what the result of their action might be, nor how to justify it intellectually, certain only that they were directed by the Holy Spirit.

This seems to us very disturbing and dangerous. It looks like acting upon the impulse of the moment. "First act, then think," sounds strange doctrine in the ears of men like ourselves brought up to live very much within the bounds of the proverb, "Look before you leap." But there are two points at which men may look before they leap; one without

and one within, or one above and one below; and the proverb suggests to us rather the outward and the below than the
inward and the above. The apostles did not act thought-
lessly, because they did not base their action upon a nice
calculation of the probable consequences. To calculate consequences and to act solely with a view to consequences, is
worldly wisdom. The apostles were not guided in their action by worldly wisdom. They were guided by the Spirit.
Care and wisdom are as clearly shown in consideration of
the source as in consideration of the probable result of an
action. It was this care and wisdom which the apostles
showed. They did not consider consequences so much as
sources. The important question was not what result would
follow, but from what source did the action spring. Per-
suaded that they were guided by the Spirit, they acted, and
the result proved their wisdom.

This also was their defense when they were attacked. This was the ground upon which the whole body
approved of the action of one of their number. When the
Jews in Jerusalem disputed with St Peter concerning his action in going to the house of Cornelius, St Peter's answer
was not to allay the anxiety of his opponents with regard to
the possible consequences of his action, but to reassert the
source of the action. He recounted his vision, he maintained
that the Holy Spirit sent him, he declared that God gave the
Holy Spirit to Cornelius and his household. His action was
necessary. "What was I, that I could withstand God?"
(11:17). Convinced of the source of his action, the Council at
once upheld it.

Similarly, St Paul defended his action before the Jerusalem Council. He had nothing to say of consequences
possible or probable. He strove to convince his hearers that
he had acted under the guidance of the Holy Spirit. To the
apostles and elders he declared "all things that God had
done with them" (15:4); to the multitudes he declared
"what signs and wonders God had wrought among the Gen-

tiles by them" (15:12). Signs and wonders were enough to prove to the multitude that God was with them; for all believed that "no man can do these signs except God be with him." The source of his action was more important than the probable consequences which worldly wisdom could foresee. When his hearers were convinced of the source of his action, opposition broke down. The leaders of the church accepted it and approved it.

Today we are more anxious about consequences, less sure of sources. When new and strange action is proposed, or actually effected, and questions are asked, the first question is, Is it wise? What will be the result of permitting such things to be done? We hear men argue, If we allow such and such actions to pass uncondemned the Church will have denied her faith, or her orders, or her sacraments, and the faith will be overthrown, the orders cease, the sacraments be destroyed. This was the sort of judgment which the apostles refused to admit. Only one other judgment is possible, and that is the judgment of the Spirit which led to the action. From this judgment the Church today shrinks. The Christian body does not seem to feel sure of its ground. Men say, We can judge actions: these are open. In judging these they seem to feel that they are dealing with something concrete. They feel at home with what they call facts; but the spirit which impelled the action seems to be something intangible and rather nebulous. They do not feel sure of themselves in dealing with that. If Christians take some unusual line of conduct and say, We felt impelled by the Spirit of God to do this, voices are heard on all sides, crying of precedents, and consequences. None seems to dare to inquire by what Spirit these men were impelled to their action. But this was the one question with which the apostles were wholly concerned in such a case.

When we turn from considerations of Spirit to considerations of policy and expediency we base our judgment upon the unknown; we forsake the way of the Spirit; we are in danger of losing the path which leads to the revelation of truth.

Of the results of action we are not capable judges. The Council of Jerusalem could not have foretold the results which would follow upon its decisions. St Paul himself could not foresee the results which would follow his journey to Jerusalem. Results are seldom exactly what we expect; they are often very different from our expectations. We assert boldly that such and such consequences will follow; they very seldom do. The man who anticipates with any approach to accuracy the consequences of any critical action is justly admired as a wonderful prophet. To base our judgment upon anticipation of consequences is to base it upon the most unstable foundations.

And the sure foundation we reject. Nowhere is the Spirit revealed as the Spirit who guides men by enabling them to anticipate the results of their action. Once and again the Spirit inspired prophets to foretell coming events so that the servants of God might prepare to take the right action when the event actually came to pass; never did He cause men to foresee what the providence of God would cause to result from their action. But constantly, again and again, He inspired them to judge the spirit behind actions done. St Peter so judged the spirit of the lame man at the Beautiful Gate, and of Ananias and of Simon Magus; so Stephen judged the spirit of his opponents; so the apostles chose men full of the Holy Spirit; so St Paul judged the spirit which moved Elymas to oppose the conversion of the proconsul; and so the Council of Jerusalem judged the spirit which moved St Peter and St Paul when their actions seemed questionable. St John indeed exhorts Christians to try the spirits. In truth, this is the one thing that Christian men can judge. Spirit answers to spirit. Christian men inspired by the Holy Ghost can know the spirit which inspires such and such a man to do such and such an action. The Spirit was given to the Church that the Church might so judge spiritually spiritual things. To decline to question the spirit and to give our whole attention to the material form is to depart from the Spirit.

But it will perhaps be objected that we cannot be bound to approve every action which good men perform from high motives. Certainly we cannot. It is one thing to recognize that good men, moved by good motives, often do foolish, or even wrong, things; it is another to decline to appeal to the Spirit, preferring to base our judgments rather upon imagined consequences than upon recognition of spiritual guidance. Some actions are at once apparent: they could not be the result of the Holy Spirit's inspiration. Some are in doubt. It is these that we are to judge and to support or to oppose. My point is, that in arriving at a decision in a question of doubt, the apostles in the Acts were guided solely by their sense of the Spirit behind the action, not by any speculations as to consequences which might ensue.

And so they found the truth. Gradually the results of the action manifested themselves, and, seeing them, they perceived what they had really done, and learnt the meaning of the truth revealed in the action. But if, from fear of the consequences, they had checked or forbidden the action, they would have lost this revelation. They would have missed the way to truth. And that is the danger which besets judgments based upon expediency, or upon anticipations of results. Such judgments close the way to the revelation of new truth. The unknown is too fearful, the untried too dangerous. It is safer to refuse than to admit. So the possibility of progress is lost, and the opportunity. From this the apostles were saved by their recognition of the supremacy of the Spirit.

PART III

CONTEMPORARY ISSUES

The role of the Holy Spirit in missions may be said to encompass everything that is done. As Roland Allen noted, the apostles were saved from any loss of progress in mission by "their recognition of the supremacy of the Spirit." However, recognizing the truth of these statements and translating it into issues with which we deal on a daily basis seems to require differing degrees of insight. This section is an example of both the issues and the care which is necessary to understand the work of the Spirit.

Peter Wagner's personal pilgrimage sets out the context of the discussion in this section. Wagner provides a reflective look at the change in his theological paradigm from the early days of serving in Bolivia to his current worldwide ministry. Wagner was invited to present a paper at the 1996 EMS conference largely due to the global influence he has within the missions community. True to form, Dr. Wagner provided both an insightful and missiologically challenging paper. He has the unique ability to take us all to the edge of our comfort zones and produce deeply felt responses, while maintaining an exemplary degree of civility toward everyone. He is truly a remarkable person.

After Wagner's presentation at the conference, four individuals presented verbal responses covering a wide range of concerns and insights directed primarily to Wagner. While the responses were helpful, it was decided that each of the four would be asked to take one aspect of their comments and prepare an article which addresses the specific issues and not just Wagner's position. As a guideline, they were asked to use Wagner's paper as a case study from which to build their contribution. The issues to be addressed included the broader issues of spiritual dynamics and how

105

we discuss them (Moreau), the epistemological foundations (Priest), the hermeneutical foundations (Orme), and the philosophical issues (Van Rheenen). Each author agreed to cover the issues assigned and the results are included here.

The intention of this section was to introduce the kind of "careful and irenic scrutiny" which Gary McGee called for in his paper. The editor sent copies of each of the four articles to Dr. Wagner for his comment and response, should he so desire. However, with the pressures of a heavy teaching and travel load, Wagner decided to forego any further response. Although the process was not perfect, it does provide us with a means of trying to achieve the ideal which we are calling for within the EMS. All the contributors deserve our gratitude for opening the dialogue, while the rest of the community must continue to discuss the issues they raise.

6

CONTEMPORARY DYNAMICS OF THE HOLY SPIRIT IN MISSIONS: A PERSONAL PILGRIMAGE

C. Peter Wagner

Receiving the invitation to present this paper was at once a pleasant and a humbling experience. I say "humbling" because I will be the first to recognize that I have not been paying my dues to the Evangelical Missiological Society in recent years as I should have. While I have faithfully sent in my annual financial contribution, I have not paid the more costly dues of attending the annual meetings, and therefore I deserve an invitation to make a presentation much less than most of my colleagues who are here with us today. I say "pleasant" because I am delighted that the EMS has made a dialogue on the Holy Spirit in missions the major theme for the regional meetings this past year. I think this is a crucial issue not only for this year, but even increasingly so for the foreseeable future in world missions.

There are several approaches I could take in addressing the topic to which I have been assigned. Of them all, the one that I feel will provide the best platform for raising the issues in this particular meeting is a description and analysis of my personal pilgrimage in getting more in touch with the power of the Holy Spirit in missions than I previously had been. However, as a prelude to that, I feel it would be worthwhile to spend a few moments in suggesting a biblical framework.

The Holy Spirit as an "Advantage"

Some biblical scholars would say that the events described in Matthew 16 are the most important events in Jesus' public ministry between his baptism and his crucifixion. As the narrative unfolds, Jesus' disciples had been in his personal company for about a year and a half. That is when Jesus chose to ask them the question: "Who do men say that I, the Son of Man, am?" After they mentioned John the Baptist, Elijah, and others, Jesus asked, "But who do you say that I am?" When Peter responded for the group, "You are the Christ, the Son of the living God," it was the first time they had really verbalized their conclusion that Jesus was truly the Messiah that the Jewish people had been waiting for.

It was only after they knew for sure who he was that Jesus could then tell them why he came to earth: "On this rock I will build my church." This is the first time that Jesus uses the word "church." And when he did, in the same breath he told them that the growth of the church around the world would inevitably involve spiritual warfare. He said, "and the gates of Hades shall not prevail against it." The obvious implication is that the gates of Hades would, indeed, attempt to stop the growth of the church, but that they would not be successful. Why? Because Jesus immediately said to his disciples, "I will give you the keys of the kingdom of heaven."

The gates of Hades apparently can be opened with certain "keys" which will allow the advance of the kingdom of heaven to occur through the building of the church. What, then are the keys that Jesus was giving his disciples? "Whatever you bind on earth will be bound in heaven." Binding apparently can make way for the spread of the gospel, or for what later would be described as world missions. Shortly before this incident at Caesarea Philippi, Jesus had prepared his disciples by using that same verb, *deo,* when he said, "how can one enter a strong man's house and plunder his goods, unless he first *binds* the strong man?" (Matt 12:29). It could well be, therefore, that "binding the strong man" could have something significant to do with removing obstacles to world evangelization and to the advance of the kingdom of God.

But back to Matthew 16. As soon as Jesus told his disciples that they would have the keys of the kingdom of heaven, he went on to inform them that they would have to be using these keys without his presence. It was a bombshell when he first broke the news to them that he would soon leave, so much of a bombshell that Peter got into a serious argument with the Master and received some of Jesus' harshest words, "Get behind me, Satan!"

When the dust from that first shock settled, however, Jesus calmly explained to them why it was necessary that he leave them. We do not find this in Matthew 16, but in John 14 and 16. Jesus tells them that they will have an *advantage* by not having him present. But what could possibly be an advantage over having the Son of God, the second person of the Trinity, physically present with them? Jesus explains in this way: "Nevertheless, I tell you the truth. It is to your advantage that I go away; for if I do not go away, the Helper will not come to you" (John 16:7). Jesus seems to be teaching that the disciples would be *better off* with the immediate presence of the third person of the Trinity than they would be with the second person, at least for the task of building the church or spreading the gospel around the world.

This is why, when the time came for Jesus actually to leave, he told his disciples not to go off preaching the gospel. They certainly had been thoroughly trained and equipped and commissioned to do that very thing after three years with the Master. But Jesus told them that they must not start evangelistic campaigns or missionary work. Instead they were to "tarry in the city of Jerusalem." Until when? Until "you are endued with power from on high" (Luke 24:49). To underscore this, Jesus saved these for his very last recorded words to the disciples: "But you shall receive power when the Holy Spirit has come upon you; and you shall be witnesses to Me in Jerusalem, and in all Judea and Samaria, and to the end of the earth" (Acts 1:8).

The disciples obeyed Jesus, the Holy Spirit came on Pentecost, and they began spreading the kingdom of God, a process which has steadily continued for almost 2000 years.

Dealing with the subtleties of Trinitarian theology has never been simple. Nevertheless, it seems clear that the obligation of spreading the gospel through the missionary task of the church is more directly connected with the person and work of the Holy Spirit than with the Father or with the Son, recognizing, of course, that the Holy Spirit proceeds from both the Father and the Son and that it would be erroneous to push the distinction too far. It seems fair to say, however, because Jesus Himself said it, that the immediate presence of the Holy Spirit is an advantage.

Why the Holy Spirit is a *Necessity* for Effective Mission

Not only is this an advantage, but it must be considered a *necessity* for those of us who are called to spread the gospel in today's world no less than it was a necessity for the evangelists and missionaries of the first century. Consider the implications of Jesus' statement to the disciples: "He who believes in Me, the works that I do he will do also" (John 14:12). John had just constructed the fourth Gospel around seven prominent works of Jesus including such things as turning water into wine, healing the sick, feeding 5,000, and raising the dead, just to mention some. How could Jesus' disciples do such works? Not in their human strength. Supernatural power was required. They, of course, could not become God and function with a divine nature. Jesus gave them the answer in the same verse when he said, "because I go to My Father." He immediately added: "And I will pray the Father, and He will give you another Helper" (John 14:16), the Holy Spirit.

Many times we do not see the awesome significance of this because we fail to recognize that Jesus did none of his mighty works by using the divine attributes he possessed as the second person of the Trinity. Philippians 2 informs us that he abstained from using them during his incarnation until the time that he was crucified. Jesus had already taught this to his disciples when he said, "Most assuredly I say to you, the Son can do nothing of Himself" (John 5:19), which certainly could not be a reference to his divine nature, but only to his human nature, which was his *modus operandi* while on earth. Jesus' supernatural power to do the works that he did came from the Father through the Holy Spirit. In Matthew 12, for example, where Jesus again uses the verb, *deo,* as in binding the strong man, he says, "If I cast out demons *by the Spirit of God ...*" (Matt 12:28). Such statements of Jesus could be multiplied.

As if to underscore this, Luke introduces Acts by affirming that even the commandments that Jesus gave to his apostles he gave *through the Holy Spirit* (Acts 1:2), implying that the power for such inspired words came from the *third* person of the Trinity and not directly from the divine nature of the *second* person of the Trinity. That is why, as I have said, we are to have access (although, granted, not in the same degree) to the very supernatural power that operated through Jesus for three and one half years. It is only on that basis that Jesus could expect his followers to do the same works which he did.

To Bolivia with I.F.M.A.

Although I did not grow up in a Christian home, my post-conversion formation in the faith was quite classically evangelical: Inter-Varsity Christian Fellowship; Urbana; Fuller Seminary under Wilbur Smith, Harold Lindsell, and Carl Henry; and ordination in a Bible Church associated with I.F.C.A. These credentials served to introduce me to the two I.F.M.A. missions under which my wife and I served in Bolivia for 16 years: South America Mission (then called South American Indian Mission) and S.I.M. International (then called Andes Evangelical Mission, formerly the Bolivian Indian Mission).

Ecclesiologically I had adopted two distinctive features of the party line with which I was associated: I was a separatist with a strong aversion to liberals of any kind, and I was anti-Pentecostal. Among other things, I worked closely together with Clyde Taylor of the E.F.M.A. to organize the Evangelical Association of Bolivia with the view of affiliating with the World Evangelical Fellowship.

As I look back on those years in the context of the theme of this paper, I now see clearly that I was severely handicapped in my appreciation of the dynamics of the Holy Spirit in world mission. In fact it remains a puzzle to me how I could be such a convinced biblical inerrantist and at the same time ignore or even reject large quantities of obvious biblical teaching.

Beginning the Paradigm Shift

As I recall, my first I.F.M.A. colleague who began to color outside the lines and who dared to hint in public that something like speaking in tongues just might be a work of the Holy Spirit was David Howard of the Latin America Mission when he first made contact with Gregory Landero's movement in Colombia. This was shocking because at the same time missionaries were being dismissed from I.F.M.A. missions for doing that very thing.

I was still part of the anti-Pentecostal contingent when I spent my 1967-1968 furlough studying church growth under Donald McGavran in the newly established Fuller School of World Mission. However, McGavran taught us that the best way to study church growth in any geographical area was to research the churches which are growing the fastest. In my part of the world, it so happened that the Pentecostal churches were growing much faster than any other kind. So I decided to swallow my pride and see first hand what the Pentecostals in Latin America might be doing. I was surprised to discover that their churches were filled with true believers who had at least as good an understanding of the Bible and theology as the members of our supposedly more biblical churches, who exhibited the fruit of the Spirit in their lives, but who also seemed to be in touch with a power of the Holy Spirit that was uncomfortable to many of us.

I compiled my research in a book, *Look Out! The Pentecostals Are Coming* (Creation House), although I must confess that I hedged perhaps more than I might have on the cause-and-effect relationship between the power of the Holy Spirit and the phenomenal growth of those churches. It was a small beginning to what would later develop into a major paradigm shift.

The Nudge from Herbert Kane

By now I have left Bolivia and am teaching church growth at the Fuller School of World Mission. I was no longer anti-Pentecostal, but I had put the Holy Spirit on the back burner, so to speak, during the decade of the 1970s while helping to develop and promote the Church Growth

Movement. Although debates on some of the technical principles of church growth became intense at times, progress was made, and one of the most gratifying pats on the back came at the end of the decade from Herbert Kane, a former I.F.M.A. missionary like myself and a missiologist on the faculty of Trinity Evangelical Divinity School. In his book, *The Christian Mission Today and Tomorrow* (Baker Book House), Kane dedicated a whole chapter to the Church Growth Movement and said up front that church growth "has been the most dynamic movement in mission circles in recent years" (p. 201).

But the friendly nudge came at the end of the chapter. There Kane said, "The proponents of church growth, with few exceptions, have emphasized the human factors and all but overlooked the divine factor. We need constantly to remember that ... in the words of Zechariah, it is not by might nor by power but by the Spirit of the Lord" (p. 212). My kneejerk defensive reaction was, "Hey, wait a minute! If Herb Kane really read our books carefully enough, he could find some references to the Holy Spirit—at least in the footnotes!" This makes us chuckle now because deep down we really knew that Herbert Kane was right. While we might have *assumed* that the work of the Holy Spirit was important in church growth missiology, we certainly had not dealt with it up front and in any useful detail.

Herb Kane provoked me enough to sincerely seek the Lord as to how the deficiency that he had surfaced could be remedied. I soon began to feel that God was directing me to dedicate a considerable portion of my research, writing, and teaching time in the 1980s to look into the dynamics of the Holy Spirit in world mission. As it turned out, the assignment has since extended into the 1990s, taking the shape of three distinct seasons of research and writing.

The Season of Signs and Wonders: 1980-1988

It was just about this time that John Wimber, who had been working for me at the Charles E. Fuller Institute for Evangelism and Church Growth, decided to plant a new church which later became the Anaheim Vineyard. Since we were close friends, I monitored his progress very carefully, especially when he began to pray for the sick, something that neither of us had been teaching in our church growth seminars. I personally had little problem with praying for the sick, but the plot really began to thicken when some of the sick people got well! My Quaker friend was actually practicing faith healing! I became curious enough to visit Wimber's services from time to time to observe what was going on.

Meanwhile, John was continuing to help me teach church growth in my Doctor of Ministry courses. As we were discussing our teaching plan for 1981, Wimber said, "What would you think of letting me teach a half-day session on the relationship of signs and wonders to church growth?" The risk-taking part of me replied, "Sure, why not?" Recognizing, however, that something like this had never before been taught in Fuller Seminary, I asked our dean, Paul Pierson, to come and sit through the class with me. After four hours, we were impressed. We debriefed with John at lunch that day. Among other things, John said, "I actually have enough material to teach a whole course on this!"

This initiated an intense discussion of issues related to the dynamics of the Holy Spirit in world missions in our School of Missions faculty which lasted for months. None of us, all experienced field missionaries, had come from a background which would have prepared us for the decision we eventually made to experiment with a course in our missions curriculum which would be built around the work of the Holy Spirit. But we went ahead and introduced MC510,

Signs, Wonders and Church Growth, into our 1982 schedule. I would supervise it and John Wimber would teach it.

Although virtually every member of our faculty visited the class at least once, Charles Kraft was the one who joined me in attending the whole course. By the end of the quarter we had each gone through a paradigm shift. We began as spectators and ended as participants. We were both praying for the sick regularly and actually seeing some verifiable healings taking place as we prayed.

Signs and wonders quickly rose to the top of my missiological research agenda. Given the continued explosive effectiveness of the Pentecostal movement in worldwide mission, the relationship between this work of the Spirit and the spread of the gospel became more and more evident. By 1988 I felt I had enough material to publish my findings, which I did in *How to Have a Healing Ministry in Any Church* (Regal Books).

The Season of Prayer and Spiritual Warfare: 1987-1996

Before the season of signs and wonders ended, God had begun to indicate to me that my next assignment related to the dynamics of the Holy Spirit in missions would be prayer. I did not at first relish the thought because I was afraid that, after signs and wonders, this would be a boring assignment. But I was wrong. The nine years I have now given to researching, writing, and teaching on prayer have been the most exciting years of over 40 years of ordained ministry!

Since prayer was a brand new field for me, I began by collecting as many books on prayer as I could find. I now have nine or ten shelves of them. The chief and most obvious reason for acquiring these books was to learn as much as I could about what others already knew about prayer. But an equally important reason was to discover areas which, at that time, were not adequately covered in the literature. I soon found three such areas: (1) the relationship between prayer and church growth; (2) intercession for Christian leaders; and (3) strategic-level intercession. I decided to focus my research on these three areas, which I did.

It soon became clear, as members of the Evangelical Missiological Society well know, that the third area, strategic-level intercession, would spark the most controversy. It became highlighted during the meeting of Lausanne II in Manila in 1989 in which five workshop speakers dealt with what we were calling "territorial spirits." Partially in conjunction with my new research assignment on strategic-level intercession, I left Manila knowing that I would be called upon to accept the leadership of what was later called the International Spiritual Warfare Network. Soon after that, on the invitation of Luis Bush, I brought the Spiritual Warfare Network into the A.D. 2000 United Prayer Track when I became Prayer Track coordinator in 1991.

I had by then bought into the motto of the A.D. 2000 Movement: *"A church for every people and the gospel for every person by the year 2000."* We live in an amazing missiological era in which, for the first time in history, we can see light at the end of the great commission tunnel. The present generation is the first generation ever which has the human resources, the financial resources, and the spiritual resources available to complete the task. To be honest, ours is also the first generation which has actually had the technological tools to quantify the remaining task accurately enough to know how close we really are. It seems that almost monthly I receive new information which boosts my faith that not only *can* it be done, but that it *will* be done.

Now, what does this have to do with the contemporary dynamics of the Holy Spirit in missions? Here I begin to base my conclusions on biblical and theological premises which, experience tells us, not all will agree with. I believe that the major reason why more people haven't become believers through the centuries is that the "god of this age" has successfully blinded their minds (see 2 Cor 4:3-4). Nevertheless, steady progress has been made and today Satan is backed up in what could possibly be seen as his last geographical fortress, the 10/40 Window (not denying, of course, that Satan is also much too malignantly active in virtually every other part of the world as well). George Otis, Jr.'s research has convinced me of the validity of the conclusion that Satan, the "god of this age," is perhaps more deeply and more firmly entrenched in the 10/40 Window than he may ever have been in any other part of the world. If such is the case, the advance of missions in the near future cannot be business as usual. What has been effective for spreading the gospel in the past might very well not be as effective in the future. We do not live in normal times.

I believe that both Satan and God know these things very well. On Satan's part, it causes him to have "great wrath because he knows that he has a short time" (see Rev 12:12). The power of Satan has never been more intense than it is now that we are penetrating what may be his last fortress. He is ready to go for broke, so to speak.

On God's part, I sense that he is giving to his people some relatively new spiritual insights with which most of us have not been familiar in the past. He may be giving to world missions the greatest power boost since the time he sent William Carey to India and began the modern missionary movement. The missionary task, which Jesus described to Paul as taking the *ethne* (or the unreached people groups) "from the power of Satan to God" (see Acts 26:18) is, in my mind, a clear commission to bare-fisted spiritual warfare. And since the primary biblical weapon of spiritual warfare is prayer, the understanding and advocacy of this new spiritual technology falls directly into the research area I have been assigned.

As I have worked on this for seven years, I have concluded that the three primary areas of this new spiritual insight for completing the great commission, which we have largely ignored until this present decade, are: (1) strategic-level spiritual warfare, (2) spiritual mapping, and (3) identificational repentance. I am completing a six-volume "Prayer Warrior" series of books which will total about 1500 pages by way of reporting to the body of Christ what I have been learning in this second season of research into the contemporary dynamics of the Holy Spirit in missions. The two which relate most directly to the controversial area of strategic-level intercession are *Warfare Prayer* and *Confronting the Powers*, the latter of which was offered earlier this year by Regal Books as a gift to all members of the Evangelical Missiological Society who requested a copy.

A Parallel Stream: The Book of Acts 1982-1995

As might be expected from a missiologist with a specialty in church growth, my favorite book in the Bible would be the book of Acts. This was my textbook for 13 years as I taught the 120 Fellowship of Lake Avenue Congregational Church Sunday after Sunday. For back-up resources, I have acquired a library of commentaries on Acts and related material which covers about six feet of shelf space. As I was moving through the first two seasons of research into the contemporary dynamics of the Holy Spirit in missions, I was also engaged in an intense and prolonged study of the one book of the Bible which deals in most depth with the subject.

In the course of time, something became clearer and clearer to me. Virtually every commentary I had been using agreed that the theme outline verse for the whole book of Acts was Acts 1:8: "You shall receive power when the Holy Spirit has come upon you; and you shall be witnesses to Me in Jerusalem, and in all Judea and Samaria, and to the end of the earth." The two major elements in Acts, then, were power ministries and cross-cultural missiology. However, none of the classical commentaries that filled my six-foot shelf was written by one who had accumulated professional expertise in power ministries and in missiology. By then, however, by the providence of God I had built a bit of an academic track record of teaching courses in both subjects on a graduate level. Given the questions which were surfacing in my parallel research, it is understandable that I would become more and more frustrated at what I was not finding in my shelf of resources. I began seeing things in Acts directly relating to the dynamics of the Holy Spirit in missions that I could find in none of my commentaries.

This led me to consider writing a commentary myself. I first did a library search and found that we already had 1,398 commentaries on Acts in English. This gave me pause, but I nevertheless decided that commentary number 1,399 was justified mainly because I considered that something more specifically dealing with the contemporary dynamics of the Holy Spirit in missions in Acts should be available to those who cared about this matter. Regal Books published three volumes, totaling over 700 pages called, *Spreading the Fire, Lighting the World,* and *Blazing the Way.*

The Season of the New Apostolic Reformation:
1993 Onward

It was sometime in 1993 that a church growth phenomenon I had been observing on all continents took on a new dimension for me. I suddenly realized that I was observing the most radical change in the way of doing church in world Christianity since the Protestant Reformation! This movement, which, (after experimenting with several other names including "postdenominationalism"), I have come to call the New Apostolic Reformation, was exhibiting the fastest rate of church growth around the world. Also, equally interesting to me, these churches seemed to be combining the technical aspects of church growth on which I had been concentrating in the 1970s and 1980s with the spiritual aspects of church growth on which I had been concentrating in the 1980s and the 1990s in a more overt and creative way than any other type of churches I had previously seen.

This caused me to enter into a new season of research, writing, and teaching which, now that I am 66 years of age, might conceivably be my last. But it seems to be shaping up as a culmination and a synthesis of all that I have done over the last 26 years in the missiological academy.

I have actually composed the entire first draft of this paper in a hotel room here in Thailand in the heart of the 10/40 Window. Thailand—previously known as a virtually impenetrable realm of Buddhism, of spirit houses, of the international industry of recreational sex—has recently become a bright spot for the kingdom of God. I am participating, along with almost 10,000 others, in the annual conference of the Hope of God International, a New Apostolic Reformation church planting movement headed up by Kriengsak Chaeronwongsak, Ph.D., a professor of economics in the university and author of twelve textbooks in his field. Although veteran missionaries told him it couldn't be done, he has now planted 366 churches in Thailand, he expects 790 by this time next year, and his goal is 80,000 Hope of God churches in Thailand by 2015. Concomitantly, he has announced that he believes that, by 2015, there will be Hope of God "seed churches" in all 224 of the world's nations and territories. He now has 30 churches planted in 16 of the 224 nations. Kriengsak's movement seems to me to combine the best of what I have been learning about strategies of church multiplication as well as the contemporary dynamics of the Holy Spirit in missions.

I mention this principally to record one of the numerous case studies that I am collecting on the New Apostolic

Reformation. Fuller Seminary held a National Symposium for its leaders in May, and the seminary has approved a new course, Churches of the New Apostolic Paradigm, which will first be offered in June 1997. In the course we will elaborate on historical roots of this movement such as the African Independent Churches, the Chinese house churches, the Latin American grass roots churches, and the U.S. independent charismatic churches. We will discuss major changes taking place in such areas as name, structure, leadership training, focus, worship style, prayer forms, financing, power paradigm, and most apropos to this meeting, outreach, including church planting and world missions.

For most churches of the New Apostolic Reformation, the contemporary dynamics of the Holy Spirit in missions is not regarded merely as an interesting item for dialogue in a professional society. It is for them, here and now, a principal and nonnegotiable ingredient in effectively reaching a lost world for Jesus Christ. As a matter of fact, it might be well, once we have finished debating to what extent and what forms the power of the Holy Spirit should or should not take in planning our missionary strategy, to consider dedicating prime time in future meetings like this to learn how it is actually being implemented by the leaders of what might well turn out to be the missiological wave of the future.

7

BROADENING THE ISSUES: HISTORIOGRAPHY, ADVOCACY, AND HERMENEUTICS: RESPONSE TO C. PETER WAGNER

A. Scott Moreau

Introduction

I must begin this response by expressing my gratitude on behalf of many in the missions community to Peter Wagner for constantly keeping us on our toes, always finding the new frontiers and never being satisfied with the *status quo*. He has been on the cutting edge of several "missiological blades" throughout his career and those of us who might be more inclined to stay where we are have not been able to push our roots of complacency too deeply. For the fact that he has not let us sit back either theologically or praxeologically we as a missions community are deeply grateful.

Because others in this volume are focusing on the epistemological and hermeneutical issues, in my response I will concentrate on the following: 1) the use of a personal pilgrimage as a way of explaining a historical trend, 2) the use of reporting and advocating within a framework of terminology which asserts itself as scholarship, 3) new interpretations and the hermeneutical community, and 4) the idea of "spiritual technology."

Narrative Historiography: The Personal Pilgrimage

Wagner's paper on the work of the Spirit in missions is a narrative of his theological development. It presents *his* story, the story of God's work in his life and thinking over the past several decades, and we recognize personal testimony as *one* of the important tools to investigate the work of the Spirit in missions. After all, the story of the work of the Spirit is the story of the work of the Spirit *through people*. However, history as autobiography (or, in this case, autobiography as history) will *always* have inherent weaknesses. History is more than just the collection of autobiography; it is the interweaving of the work of God through the lives of individuals, families, peoples, nations, and continents. It is more than just the stories; it is the interpretation of those stories into the larger pattern of events. None of us, it is true, enjoys God's perspective on the tapestry he is weaving. We are called, however, to work together as a Spirit-led community to develop his perspective. No one person can claim to have the whole story, and every person must be willing to participate within the Spirit-led community's perception.

In this larger context it can be seen that critiquing autobiography is notoriously difficult. How can one critique personal experiences and the sense of God's leading in an individual's life? It is almost impossible to focus on the personal experiences themselves, and the intention must never be to denigrate the person whose testimony is being evaluated. However, any attempt to uncover the implicit principles and methodologies inherent in the use of the experiences within the autobiography, their interpretation, and their meaning in contexts may have the look and feel of inappropriate personal attack. Thus, to say that responding to personal narrative is a subjective exercise is to seriously understate the difficulty of the problem!

Specifically in this regard, the inherently anecdotal nature of Wagner's approach demonstrates that narrative can only supplement, and can never replace, the investigative methods of history, the social sciences, and theology which have stood the test of time. This is not naively returning to Enlightenment thinking. Rather, it is recognizing that if truth is our standard, and our thinking is challenged on the argument that our worldview is flawed, then we must identify and use tools which will help us to determine what is truth and how to construct an appropriate worldview. Every person committed to the truth of the Scriptures has already, by extension, committed himself or herself to this. Scripture is the ultimate tool, and we are to submit ourselves to the worldview it portrays. This is not done just as individuals, however, but as individuals in community.

Thus, while we deeply appreciate Wagner's story, and we see it as part of the total work of God within the world church, we are not released from submitting his claims and interpretations to the truths found in Scripture and seen through history. Since worldviews and truth claims are being challenged, we are indeed foolish if we do not use whatever tools we have at our disposal to investigate the challenges being leveled.

On a more general level, the perils of using what essentially amounts to anecdotal narrative apply not only to what Wagner says, but to anyone who uses such an approach to establish broad-ranging historical or contemporary analysis. Unfortunately, recent deconstructionist attacks on traditional historiography and some of the more radical approaches to the sociology of knowledge have tended to reduce the study of history to gathering a collection of personal narratives. The fact remains that a Christian perspective on history is that it is far more than just a collection of personal narratives—it is the confluence of those narratives within varied community contexts, all in the larger scope of God's purposes and work in the world. While we recognize and need to benefit from the validity of certain elements of the deconstructionist critique or our ability to be "objective," at the same time we cannot capitulate to reducing history (or truth) to narrative from a personal perspective.

Reporting, Advocacy, and Scholarship?

Wagner relates that much of his recent work has been God's assignment to him to "report" or "publish . . . findings" as well as to be an advocate of signs and wonders, prayer (and especially strategic level spiritual warfare [SLSW]), and, most recently, the New Apostolic Reformation paradigm. A significant concern of mine is that what Wagner says is *merely* reporting and advocacy many readers *perceive to be* academic scholarship. He increases the possibility of this confusion by using a variety of terms throughout his paper which blend the ideas together: researching, observing, reporting, advocating, writing, involved in scholarship, intense and prolonged study, and the missiological academy. Such language leads the reader not to see what Wagner is doing as merely reporting and advocating, but gives an air of scholarly, objective research which is not supported by the style of work which Wagner himself purports to set out. It should not be surprising, then, that when scholars do respond they are sharply critical.

An inherent problem with reporting and advocating is that biblical support, when sought, will be agenda-driven and skewed by the researcher's desire to find texts which say what he or she wants them to say. As a result, such meanings are easier to read into the texts. The difference between going to the biblical text to *discover* the truth and going to the biblical text to *confirm* what we want to advocate as truth is significant. The *confirming* agenda can result in the worst form of proof-texting in which passages are given meanings not supported by grammar, literary style, or context. Wagner's works, such as his three volume commentary on Acts (1994, 1995a, 1995b), are challenged on this very issue by Priest, Mullen, and Campbell in their chapter in *Spiritual Power and Missions* (1995).

Especially in the case of SLSW, the potential is dangerous. Wagner reports many positive anecdotes of what is happening. There are negative ones as well. For example, an Indian friend tells me that he spends considerable time and energy putting out the "spiritual fires" caused by well-meaning but culturally ignorant Christians who visit India and engage in public prayer walks and attempts to cast down territorial spirits. Ready to engage in power encounters without engaging the culture deeply, they come on hit-and-run forays leaving behind no fruit and confused non-Christians. My friend has Hindus telling him that they are surprised to find out that Christians are no different from Hindus in their use of magic and belief in spirits, citing the prayer walkers as proof of their contention. They feel that the dividing line between Christianity and Hinduism is far thinner than they had previously thought, and see no reason to consider the claims of Christ as in radical opposition to their current religious system. Such "power encounters" can only be considered as "power failures" if the goal of these activities is binding the spirits of a geographic location in order to increase effective evangelism. My point is not that prayer walks are ineffective or that they should be canceled. Wagner has been very good at reporting the positive results of such efforts. One problem is that no negative cases are discussed. A second is that even the positive cases are subject to interpretation based on presuppositions and agenda (see Priest, Campbell and Mullen, pp. 40, 46-49). Because of the reporting and advocating methodology Wagner follows, the reader is left with the false impression that there are no problems with SLSW. The case study approach, like the narrative approach, has a role to play. Its role, however, must be seen as limited to the strengths and weaknesses in the methodology used in choosing and reporting the cases. As with recent political elections in the United States, the question of "spin control" is crucial, and when the control is used to ignore, downplay, or reinterpret the cases, the conclusions will of necessity be as flawed as the method used in reaching them.

One final, and significant, comment may be made. It can be readily observed in Wagner's writings that when he does respond to the critics, he does so *without letting the readers know who those critics are* (e.g., Wagner, 1996, p. 82). He reports that this is because God clearly told him in 1980 not to engage in polemics anymore (1996, p. 35), which he interprets to mean that he should not name his critics. For example, in *Confronting the Powers*, which was written as a response to the Priest, Campbell, and Mullen paper, I have not been able to find them named anywhere in the book! Thus, those who read *Confronting the Powers* are deprived of the very work which prompted its writing. While Wagner states that he hopes to present their arguments accurately and fairly (1996, p. 35), his refusal to name those who criticize him short-circuits the process of reading both sides of a story, and demeans the readers as people who are not able to think for themselves. I agree with Wagner that mean-spirited polemics is inappropriate. This does not mean, however, that we throw out all forms of debate and abrogate our responsibility for scholarly inquiry into controversial issues.

Of perhaps greater concern in this is that Wagner *does* occasionally cite some who criticize him—but only where they agree with him.[1] This selective form of citation, unfortunately, leads the reader to think that those cited ac-

---

[1]For example, Wagner cites Arnold on historic and exegetical points in which Arnold's interpretations lend strength to Wagner's argument (Wagner, 1996, pp. 209, 210, 216, 222). Where Arnold disagrees with Wagner, as in the interpretation of the powers of Eph 6:12 as territorial spirits, he is not cited. Further, Arnold does not agree with Wagner's call for warfare prayer against territorial spirits as key to reaching the world, but the reader would never know this from reading *Confronting the Powers*. This is unfair to Arnold, who might be inappropriately seen as a supporter of Wagner's conclusions (see Arnold, 1997).

tually support Wagner's conclusions when in fact they do not. This may appear harsh to say, but I strongly feel that this type of misrepresentation simply lacks integrity.

In sum I am concerned that Wagner's reporting and advocating in writing that has the appearance of scholarly discussion, as well as his excluding of the names and sources of those who criticize him, are too easily misread by his readers not simply as *reporting* but as *presenting the results of accepted missions scholarship.* At best this is a serious misrepresentation of the scholarly missiological community to the reading public. *I plead with Wagner either to stop confusing people through combining academic jargon with reporting advocacy and let his books be seen and understood as popular and non-critical journalism, or else go back to God to request clarification on the meaning of the "no polemics" order.* I am not stating this sarcastically, but perhaps, just as Wagner has gone through various seasons in his research, the "anti-polemic" nature of his writing might also be only for a season. If not, from my perspective, it would be far better to simply ignore critics than to represent them without giving them their own voice by refusing to naming them for the reading audience.

New Interpretations and the Hermeneutical Community

To preface this discussion, I note two examples of what I see as a trend in Wagner's writings. First, in *Confronting the Powers* (pp. 147-8) he proposes that Beelzebub is a territorial spirit mistakenly taken as Satan by biblical scholars. He argues that a reason scholars have not recognized that Beelzebub is a territorial spirit is that they are blinded by worldview and lack of genuine experience in the occult. Their worldview is Enlightenment-derived and tends to overlook the existence of spiritual forces and, as a result, they have not studied the occult. Due to this lack, they are not aware that Beelzebub is well known in occultic circles, and in those circles he is not identified with Satan, but with a high ranking evil spirit. Wagner contends that the Bible does not give us clear exegetical evidence that Beelzebub and Satan are to be identified (and the same goes for Wormwood [Rev. 8:11] and Abaddon [Rev. 9:11]). His argument is that it is the *presuppositions* of biblical scholars that the two are to be identified which leads them astray. Noting that we can at times be helped by the knowledge of those who are not of the church, and that (in this case), occult practitioners *know* that Satan is not Beelzebub, Wagner argues that their opinion is to be given greater weight than that of biblical scholars in understanding who Beelzebub is.

Second, also in *Confronting the Spirits*, he notes that he is uniquely qualified to write the 1399th commentary on Acts because (in addition to teaching it for 15 years) he has been trained and prepared by the Spirit in both power ministry and cross-cultural missiology (pp. 162-3). In that context, and recognizing that other interpretations are possible (p. 163), he proposes that there are five encounters in Acts with territorial spirits that no one else (to my knowledge) has previously recognized as territorial spirit encounters (1994, pp.217-221; 1995a, pp. 131, 154-57; 1995b, pp. 67-68, 170-79; 1996, pp. 161-224). A careful reading of the arguments made that these are territorial spirits, however, shows that in all five instances the arguments are all presuppositional rather than exegetical. In each case, it is *assumed* that the spirits discussed are territorial and then the discussion proceeds as though the point has been proven rather than simply assumed.

Thus, Wagner proposes new interpretations of Beelzebub and the existence of previously unseen SLSW in Acts. Through the autobiographical method of his paper, he presents this as his perception of the contemporary dynamics of the work of the Spirit in missions. The issue we face concerns not just whether Wagner's conclusions are correct, but whether this is truly the Spirit's leading and how we are to answer that question. Thus, we are back to the question raised in the first section of this response.

Paul Hiebert articulates the need for the hermeneutical community (1994, p. 91) to guide interpretive discussion. The difficulty is in finding the appropriate hermeneutical community, and this is where the rub lies. Wagner, by being a member of the conservative evangelical academy, is read by many to represent what that academy is saying. However, many, if not most of us in the academy, are not in agreement with Wagner's methods and advocacy, especially in regard to SLSW. At the same time, there is a large hermeneutical community, many of whom are activists in mission circles, who are in agreement with Wagner and who are pushing ahead of him in implementing experimental strategies designed to discover and destroy demonic strongholds over cities, peoples, and nations.

This being the case, what role does a community of faith (in this case, evangelical missiology) play when someone who comes from within it changes his or her thinking and begins to advocate unique or novel ideas as coming from the Spirit's leading? What difference does it make that an alternate hermeneutical community (in this case, more Pentecostal-oriented mission activists) embraces these ideas? Is it true that the academic non-Pentecostal community needs the paradigm shift that Wagner embraces?[2] Or is his interpretation and advocacy something which the church community in history will judge as aberrant?

To answer that question, we must consider which criteria for evaluating new theologies and methodologies have stood the test of time through history. Several may be noted, including epistemological strength, exegetical accu-

---

[2] In saying this, we must note that some non-Pentecostals agree with Wagner, and some Pentecostals disagree with him. This should not be stereotyped as a Pentecostal vs. non-Pentecostal issue.

racy, and historical confirmation by the body of the church. The questions of epistemology and exegesis are being discussed by other writers in this volume (see also the first two chapters of Rommen, 1996). They will continue to be addressed for the foreseeable future. The question of historical judgment will only be answered through the passage of time.

Wagner's implication through his testimony is that this is the leading of the Spirit. He, together with us, would affirm the biblical injunction to test the spirits (1 John 4:1-4) or the prophecies (1 Cor 14:29; 1 Thess 5:19-21). The fact that we are to evaluate new theologies presupposes some appropriate form of polemics. When Wagner has been directed not to engage in polemics, but simply to report and advocate, how then are we as a community to test the spirits without challenging or contravening God's apparent leading in his life? This is where the general principle of Scripture is that both the individual and the community are to submit to the Word of God as the final arbiter of disagreement. For example, a key question on which Wagner is being challenged is whether his apparent discovery of five instances of SLSW in Acts and subsequent claims of our need to be involved in waging spiritual warfare against territorial spirits is adequately justified in the text (see Arnold, 1997). To date I do not know of a single biblical scholar who supports Wagner's conclusions, and he readily admits that he does not find any commentaries which address the issues the way he does (1996, pp. 162-63).

Spiritual Technology

The last point I will discuss is Wagner's use of the term "spiritual technology," which has intrigued me since I first came across it in his writings. However, it is both intriguing *and* haunting, bringing to my mind echoes of C. S. Lewis' concept of the "materialist magician" (1961, p. 33).

On one side I see some in the field of missiology telling us that Western thinking, worldview, and approaches to life are unbiblical in that they drive us to overlook the territory of the demonic. We are encouraged to jettison our Enlightenment paradigms because they bifurcate spiritual and secular in unbiblical fashion, and blind us to the biblical reality of the spirit realm. With this I agree. Where I have trouble is in combining the word "technology" with the word "spiritual" in the sense that mapping territorial spirits borrows the best from both worlds. I am concerned that we may actually be borrowing the worst.

I do not want to be seen as splitting inconsequential theological hairs (which, after all, is a stereotyped hallmark of a Western approach to life and theology!). In one sense it is the terminology that is worrisome. My larger concern is not as much the term as it is that the term displays an attitude of willingness to borrow vocabulary or ideas out of context, give them a new context, and expect that they will fit hand-in-glove together. All of us would agree that we should pursue the spiritual and that we want to carefully pursue an appropriate use of technology. But combining the terms in a syncretistic neologism, however, we create something that, while looking like both, carries connotations which go beyond the intentions of either. At best it shows that we need to research the issues Wagner is pursuing. At worst, however, it may show a blend of Enlightenment ("technology") with magical ("spiritual") thinking in a mixture that is essentially unworkable. Our new advocates of SLSW may become a new set of "technocrats" blindly following a technology simply because they are captivated by the construct rather than being biblically discerning about the issues involved (see Postman, 1992).

Broader Implications:
The Ongoing Leading of the Spirit in Missions

All of this points us back to the broader issue of the role of the Holy Spirit in leading us in the missionary task today. None of us doubt that he continues to lead us in the task of reaching the world for Christ, leading the church to new strategies that fit the contemporary world and take advantage of advances in technology (e.g., the Jesus Film), research (e.g., audience analysis), and techniques (e.g., Evangelism Explosion). Few of us doubt the need to get beyond the flaw of the *excluded* middle (Hiebert, 1994, pp. 189-201), but many of us rightfully fear what I have called elsewhere the flaw of the *expanded* middle (1995, p. 34), in which too much is attributed to spirits and they take on a kind of omniscience and omnipresence which is not biblically justifiable.

All of these questions raise a broader concern. As evangelicals deeply committed to mission, we can all point to people in history who went against the grain of their community and were eventually vindicated. William Carey stands as an example of this, and is one who is cited in that regard by Wagner (1996, pp. 44-45).

Through history, however, we have examples of models other than Carey. Some have had their teachings integrated into the church, some have corrected themselves, some have been rejected, and some have formed heterodox faith communities. While Carey is certainly an example of the first, other examples are not as positive. George Pember promoted a gap theory in which the souls of pre-Adamic humans became the demons who follow Satan. His ideas are in the first edition of the Scofield Bible, but were expunged in the second. William Miller predicted that Christ would return in 1843. When that failed, he changed his prediction to 1844. His teaching eventually led to the founding of the Seventh Day Adventists, a movement still not completely identified with orthodox Christianity. William Branham was a Jesus Only faith-healer whose followers believed him to be a forerunner of the return of Christ. After his death late in 1965, his body was not buried for months, as his followers expected him to rise from the dead. Today they lie outside the mainstream of the church, declaring Branham God's prophet for the last days and publishing his sermons verbatim as God's spoken Word. The recent prophecy initiated by Bang-Ik Ha of Jesus' return on October 28, 1992 at 9:00 a.m. Central Standard Time, was reportedly confirmed by thousands who experienced similar visions and words from God. When the date passed uneventfully, embarrassment, confusion and even suicide were the result.

From the historical perspective, will Wagner's championing of the new methods of SLSW stand the test of time and church acceptance? If they are off base, how do we work together to employ the epistemological and hermeneutical principles which help us all to have an appropriate means of challenging and critiquing each other without losing track of the larger goal towards which we all strive, namely obedience to the great commission?

This is the scene of contemporary evangelical missions. It is in the midst of this confusion that we must strive to work together as the larger community of Christ committed to the Scriptures, committed to the work of God through the Spirit in our midst, and committed to each other in the mutual goal of communicating Christ clearly so that peoples of every tribe, tongue, caste, language, and nationality may have the opportunity to respond to his invitation of eternal life. Towards this end we are all committed as a community; may we not lose sight of that in the debates over issues of strategy, advocacy, and scholarship!

8

SPIRITUAL WARFARE, EPISTEMOLOGY, AND THE MISSIOLOGICAL COMMUNITY

Robert J. Priest

Dr. Wagner's paper would appear to be of historic significance: a prominent missiologist announcing the completion of a period of writing and research on the topic of prayer and spiritual warfare and the commencement of research and writing on a new topic, that of "the new apostolic reformation."

I was doubtless invited to respond to Dr. Wagner with the expectation that his paper would engage issues I (and other colleagues) had raised earlier. In order to set the context for my comments, let me begin with a brief history.

At a plenary session of the 1994 annual meetings of the Evangelical Missiological Society I read a paper (co-authored with Thomas Campbell and Bradford Mullen) entitled "Missiological Syncretism: The New Animistic Paradigm." We argued that a number of contemporary missiologists have unwittingly embraced and are teaching theologically faulty assumptions about the nature of demonic power. These missiologists maintain that demonic power is tied to objects and places such that personal safety and spiritual success depend on "mapping" such demonic ties with object and place and directing our efforts either towards avoiding such objects and places or taking action to sever the demonic connection with the object or place. This is, in large part, what spiritual warfare is supposed to entail. We argued that this wrongly understands the nature of the spiritual battle in which we are engaged and leads us to focus the battle at the wrong place, with serious pastoral consequences. We argued, furthermore, that these ideas clearly contradict biblical teaching, such as that offered in I Corinthians 8 and 10 concerning meat offered to idols. We endeavored to show from the argumentation of such missiologists that extra-biblical sources are illegitimately functioning to accredit these ideas and practices.

While our paper stirred interest among many, it raised concern among others. In response to the concern expressed by those whose ideas we critiqued that they be given an opportunity to respond, the leadership of the Evangelical Missiological Society asked me and my co-authors if we would be willing to have our paper withdrawn from the scheduled volume on world religions, and published in a separate small volume in which Drs. Wagner, Kraft, and other key spokespersons for the ideas we had critiqued, would have the opportunity to respond to us. The plan, we were told, was that this volume would be published by the time of the 1995 EMS annual meeting, since it was felt that this topic would prepare the membership for the theme of the 1996 EMS annual meeting: The Holy Spirit and Missions. Since this book would be distributed a year ahead of time, EMS members would be encouraged to carry on discussion with regard to the relevant issues during the year by reading papers on the topic at regional meetings. The process would culminate at the 1996 annual meeting where there would be opportunity finally for direct interaction among us on these issues.

Despite our qualms about the proposed format, we agreed to the proposal. Dr. Kraft agreed to write a response. Dr. Patrick Johnstone added a chapter, and our paper, together with those of Dr. Kraft and Dr. Johnstone, appeared in the EMS volume *Spiritual Power and Missions: Raising the Issues*, edited by Dr. Edward Rommen. The book was printed in time for the 1995 EMS national meetings. Dr. Wagner, however, decided that he needed an entire book to respond, and opted not to participate in this format. His book *Confronting the Powers* was later offered free to all EMS members—thus providing EMS members with his response to our paper.

The issues we had raised were discussed at regional meetings of the EMS. Dr. Wagner was invited to present a paper at the 1996 EMS annual meeting, and I was asked to participate in the panel discussion which followed. Dr. Wagner's paper appropriately fit the 1996 EMS theme of "The Holy Spirit in Missions."

But for me, and perhaps for others who came to the annual meetings expecting a presentation which connected with the prior discussion, there was a measure of frustration. Dr. Wagner's narrative does acknowledge that some of his ideas on "strategic level intercession" have raised controversy, but his narrative subordinates the controversial elements, and he fails to identify exactly what the controversy is about—ending by implying that what we've really been "debating" is "to what extent" we should make use of the power of the Holy Spirit in missions. My colleagues and I who first initiated some of this debate believe that everything we do in missions should be done "to the fullest extent" in reliance on the power of the Holy Spirit. Our paper's concern was not how much to trust the power of the Holy Spirit, but rather what assumptions should be made about the nature of demonic spirits—unholy spirits. This was the focus of our critique.

Although I appreciate Dr. Wagner's zeal for the great commission, the personal sharing of his own spiritual pilgrimage, and his concern for Spirit-empowered ministry, from my perspective it seems to be rather difficult to get Dr. Wagner to respond directly to issues raised. In his book *Confronting the Powers*, a volume which he indicated was supposed to address the issues we raise, he never directly quotes us and frequently misrepresents our position. For example, he notes (65) that his position has been characterized as an "animistic paradigm," he seems to wonder what could possibly be meant, he quotes various other evangelical authors as to definitions of "animism," and he concludes (66): "I think my critics are warning me against becoming a . . . person whose *allegiance* is not to Jesus Christ alone, but to other supernatural forces" (emphasis added). This is, of course, a straw man. We never even hinted that we thought the problem was one of *allegiance* to other supernatural forces. We were very careful to explain exactly what we meant by the term—defined it carefully, and organized our whole paper around the key ideas being critiqued. It was not "animistic *allegiance*" with which we charged anyone, but with "animistic *assumptions*" about the nature of demonic power—the assumption that demonic power is linked to objects, for example, and thus that physical contact with such objects renders one vulnerable to demons—or the assumption that the way to nullify demonic power is to sever their connections with object or place.

In this paper, Dr. Wagner announces the commencement of a new research and writing agenda on his part, one which focuses on what he is calling "the new apostolic reformation." But before we look forward to this new agenda, a brief assessment of the just completed season of research and writing on the topic of spiritual warfare is in order. The following are some considerations which ought to be factored into this assessment.

First, Dr. Wagner has helped develop new ideas about the nature of demonic power and new "spiritual technologies" for confronting such. His own writings and speeches have frequently stressed the *newness* of these ideas and spiritual technologies—such as "spiritual mapping." These new ideas amount to a fundamental shift (in Wagner's words, a "paradigm shift") in our way of doing missions, of doing hermeneutics, and of approaching sanctification in the life of the believer (cf. Priest, Campbell and Mullens 1995; Kessler 1996; Barrientos Paninski 1996; Powlison 1995).

Second, because of his gifts, reputation, institutional affiliations, and prolific writing ministry Dr. Wagner is playing a strategic role in teaching and accrediting these new ideas around the world. For example, as leader of the A.D. 2000 United Prayer Track, Dr. Wagner wrote the formal position paper on prayer for the A.D. 2000 Movement, making various of his new ideas about such things as territorial spirits and spiritual mapping central to this position paper (Wagner 1996:249-262). These ideas are not moldering unused in an ivory tower. These ideas have legs. Their truth or falsity, therefore, has profound ramifications for millions.

Since Christians have had the Bible for nearly 2,000 years, how is it that Wagner is able to discover so many new truths about the demonic? The answer, quite simply, is that he is drawing on new sources—sources other than God's special revelation, the Bible—for discovering new information about demons. Pivotal to the development and defense of his new ideas is an epistemology which relies on extra-biblical sources (e.g., demons, former occultists, pagan religious beliefs, personal experiences) for acquiring new information about the nature of demonic power—information which *sola scriptura* does not give. Despite our critique (Priest, Campbell and Mullen 1995:26-31) that one should not rely on and trust demons in demonized persons to give us new information (i.e. information not already known from Scripture) about demonic realities, Wagner (1996:70) continues to insist "that we can indeed get valid information from the world of darkness." He continues to affirm that some people "have what could be likened to a spiritual Geiger counter that has a special capacity . . . to detect demonic presence, often revealing surprisingly detailed and accurate knowledge of its identity and intentions" (Wagner 1996:68). He continues to affirm that many "shamans, witch doctors, practitioners of Eastern Religions, New Age gurus or professors of the occult on university campuses" are "sincere people of integrity" who have "much more extensive knowledge of the spirit world than most Christians have" (1996:148). It is in part through his interviews with such "experts" that he learns facts that the Bible does not tell him, such as the fact that Beelzebub is the name of a high ranking demonic principality underneath Satan (1996:148ff), rather than being simply another name for Satan, as biblical scholars have traditionally thought.

This is not the place to restate our critique of Dr. Wagner's epistemology with which he discovers extra-biblical truths about demonic realities. What needs to be clear is that he has not modified his commitment to an epistemology designed for discovering extra-biblical truths about demonic realities. Indeed, he could not modify such a commitment without then needing to go back and renounce many of the new insights he has been sharing with the evangelical world, for those insights require his extra-biblical epistemology. They cannot be sustained solely on the basis of an appeal to Scripture.

I believe that the epistemological principles being articulated by Dr. Wagner are a far more serious issue even than the specific content of new ideas about demons which he develops. Those who learn the new epistemology will have learned a method for continuing to generate new truths about spiritual matters of all sorts—truths not learned from Scripture.

It has been, and continues to be, my conviction that where Dr. Wagner proclaims new truth about demonic power, truth not derived from Scripture, he is in error; that his epistemology in reaching such conclusions is flawed, and that the potential adverse consequences to the church of proceeding on such mistaken assumptions are considerable (cf. Priest, Campbell and Mullen 1995: 21-25; Barrientos Paninski 1996; Kessler 1996).

But my personal convictions are really beside the point. What matters rather, is whether the larger missiological community decides that the epistemological issues are important enough to merit the mobilization of missiological energy and reflection by the community at large. It should be remembered that missiologists comprise an academic and professional community devoted to researching and analyzing matters pertaining to the mission and advance of the church in the world. This community must be intentional about focusing its research activities and published findings on matters of timely significance to the church. Issues pertaining to the demonic in missions, and to the epistemology of how we arrive at understandings of the demonic, are of pressing concern to missions and the church, and ought to be the focus of sustained intellectual activity by missiologists. While those who are interested in these epistemological issues would do well to review our article (Priest, Campbell and Mullen 1995), Wagner's book (1996) and Kraft's article (1995) as a starting point, they should not stop there. If missiologists are to function as a community, and not just as an *ad hoc* group of individuals each pursuing "his own thing," they must take ownership of the task of working through these issues, and institutionalize that community-wide ownership.

How ought missiologists to institutionalize owner-ship of this intellectual agenda?

First, there needs to be the recognition that the issues are exceedingly complex, and require contributions by many scholars with diverse kinds of specialties. Those who are historians ought to help us gain historical perspective on the recent "spiritual warfare" movement. They could, for example, help us compare current demonologies with ones held by Christians in other times and places, or help us evaluate the ways in which "spiritual warfare" literature, of whatever persuasion, interprets church history. Biblical scholars and theologians should be asked to examine the many biblical passages (such as ones cited by Dr. Wagner in the preceding paper, ones cited in our own earlier paper, such as I Corinthians 8 and 10, and key passages such as Daniel 10 or Deuteronomy 32:8), in the light of interpretations being made of them by various contributors to the "spiritual warfare" literature. The hermeneutical and exegetical issues require careful consideration by biblical scholars. Christian anthropologists, psychologists and comparative religionists, together with biblical scholars and theologians and field practitioners, should be asked to enter into the discussion of how non-Christian religious phenomenology relates to human realities and to spiritual ontology. The reader can doubtless think of other kinds of missiological specialists with unique gifts and skills which should be brought to the discussion. The principal point of my appeal is that no single individual can hope to assess all of these diverse issues as well as can a whole community of scholars.

Second, we must not only recognize the importance of ownership of the task by a community of missiological scholars, but we must pursue activities and create forums where the task of engagement with these issues actually occurs. The EMS is to be commended for creating a forum for the issues to be aired initially, but much more could be done to ensure that the issues become more fully engaged by the community of missiologists. Regional meetings provide one forum where such issues could continue to be explored. The Evangelical Theological Society provides a forum for scholars to create sessions on their own topics, and this is one setting where missiologists could fruitfully collaborate with biblical scholars, church historians, and theologians in focused sessions which encourage ETS members to channel their efforts and expertise into engaging missiological issues. Perhaps the EMS should also explore such a structure, one which allows for groups of missiologists to create sessions on their own topics. More avenues for publishing missiological treatments of such topics need to be fostered.

Third, missiological students should be treated, not as passive containers into whom we pour knowledge, but as active junior partners in the activity of pursuing better missiological understandings. No course offerings on spiritual warfare in Bible colleges or seminaries ought to require students to read Wagner, Kraft, Anderson, Murphy, or Warner, for example, without also requiring them to read sources such as Powlison (1995), Rommen (1995), Hiebert (1994) or Moreau (1995). Otherwise we simply indoctrinate to a party line. Advanced students should be encouraged to do theses and dissertations on specific issues related to larger "spiritual warfare" debates, and to publish brief summaries of their findings. If a research agenda can be pursued intentionally over time, there will be a cumulative effect of weeding out errors and increasing our understandings in a specific area.

If any of this is to occur, we must articulate and affirm values which foster the right sorts of missiological interactions. Missiologists should be discouraged from by passing the missiological community, and simply providing their new understandings *ex cathedra* to the broader world. They should be encouraged, rather, to attempt to demonstrate the truth of their new ideas to a community of missiological peers, from whom they actively solicit substantive feedback. Missiologists need to recognize that there is an accountability for those who publish and teach. This means that everything which they affirm in print is available for others to interact with in print. Indeed, missiologists have an obligation to interact with the truth claims of their peers. Those who critique the ideas of others must take care not to attack their motives (God alone is in the position to judge the heart), only the content of their ideas. Those whose ideas are critiqued must learn to distinguish whether or not it is their ideas which are being critiqued or their motives or character. If it is their ideas being critiqued, then they should respond at the appropriate level of engaging the substance of the critique. The larger missiological community must monitor this process, working to ensure both that inappropriate attacks on motives, character, or personality do not occur, and that substantive interaction does occur. Only through healthy substantive interaction by the full community of missiologists, will the community of missiologists fulfill its rightful role of generating solidly grounded missiological understandings.

References

Barrientos Paninski, Alberto
1996 Enfoque Pastoral del Debate. In *Poder y Misión*. San José, Costa Rica: IINDEF, pp. 66-80.

Hiebert, Paul G.
1994 Biblical Perspectives on Spiritual Warfare. In *Anthropological Reflections on Missiological Issues*. Grand Rapids: Baker Book House, pp. 203-215.

Kessler, Juan
1996 Evaluacion de este Debate desde Costa Rica. In *Poder y Misión*. San José, Costa Rica: IINDEF, pp. 53-65.

Kraft, Charles
1995 "Christian Animism" or God-Given Authority? In *Spiritual Power and Missions: Raising the Issues* (edited by Edward Rommen). Pasadena, CA: William Carey Library, pp. 88-136.

Moreau, A. Scott
1995 Religious Borrowing as a Two Way Street: An Introduction to Animistic Tendencies in the Euro-

North American Context. In *Christianity and the Religions: A Biblical Theology of World Religions.* (Edited by Edward Rommen). Pasadena, CA: William Carey Library, pp. 166-183.

Powlison, David
1995 *Power Encounters: Reclaiming Spiritual Warfare.* Grand Rapids, MI: Baker Books.

Priest, Robert J., Thomas Campbell, and Bradford Mullen
1995 Missiological Syncretism: The New Animistic Paradigm. In *Spiritual Power and Missions: Raising the Issues* (edited by Edward Rommen). Pasadena, CA: William Carey Library, pp. 9-87.

Rommen, Edward, ed.
1995 *Spiritual Power and Missions: Raising the Issues.* Pasadena, CA: William Carey Library

Wagner, C. Peter
1996 *Confronting the Powers.* Ventura, CA: Regal Books.

9

IDENTIFICATIONAL REPENTANCE AND STRATEGIC SPIRITUAL WARFARE: A HERMENEUTICAL CASE STUDY

John H. Orme

Hermeneutical spirals, circles, horizons, demonic strongholds, and territories all converge when the role of the Holy Spirit in missions is discussed. In spite of the fact that we agree on so much of the Holy Spirit's person and work, confusion and debate reign because of varying definitions, perceptions, and exegetical procedures. Particularly in hermeneutics, the evangelical world is at sea, as evidenced by the endless stream of articles and monographs. (See works cited by Thomas 1996 and McQuilkin and Mullen 1997.)

A complicating issue is that formerly special revelation was limited to the Bible alone, but now broader, experimental-observational, and anecdotal knowledge is increasingly accepted on the functional level equal to that of special revelation. (Erickson 1997: 136-140, Deere 1996, Wagner 1996, Grudem, 1988, Kraft 1979, 1995:103-117).

While this essay will not include the complex philosophical issues involved in hermeneutics, semantics, and language itself, the practical issues in missions praxis are no less complex. Indeed, apart from the gospel message itself, there can hardly be a more critical issue than the work of the Holy Spirit in removing Satanic blindness (2 Cor 4:3-6). Just how the Spirit does this and what the Scriptures teach is an intensely theological and yet practical issue.

It is only fair to grant the proposition that evangelical missionaries desire to be loyal to the Word of God and to Christ. However, C. Peter Wagner in his defense of the highly debated issues of identificational repentance, and spiritual mapping can be read as challenging this proposition. He states:

> In this book, I am not claiming biblical *proof* for the validity of strategic-level spiritual warfare, spiritual mapping or identificational repentance. I will, however, claim that we do have sufficient biblical *evidence* to warrant:
> 1. At the *least*, a working hypothesis that we can field test, evaluate, modify and refine;
> 2. At the *most*, a significant relatively new spiritual technology God has given us to meet the greatest challenge to world missions since William Carey went to India more than 200 years ago. If this is the case, refusing to use it on the part of some might be to run the risk of unfaithfulness to the Master. (1996: 89)

While not claiming absolute proof, Wagner's language and argumentation in the book strongly point toward his claim number two (2.) above. That these claims are largely supported by a hermeneutical-exegetical practice and an epistemological (revelatory) basis is not generally seen in conservative evangelical circles.

While fellow evangelical Wagner hopefully would not press the extreme of his words, "unfaithfulness to the Master," his journalistic style points toward extremes by use of illustrations such as the bedroom (intimacy with God) vs. the battlefield dichotomy (confronting the powers) (1996: 37,48). This false distinction can mislead believers who want nothing less than faithfulness to Christ and to his Word as they combine intimacy with the Lord and activism in his harvest.

To minimize this tension, Wagner suggests that we are in the same debate arena as that of the secondary issues of modes of baptism, days of worship, and celebrating

Christmas and Easter. However, the issues are not so secondary when matters of the Trinity are included (1996: 84, 87, 162). We must determine what Scripture teaches and we must arrive at conclusions just as classic debates in the past have done, always basing our conclusion on the basis of what the Scriptures teach. To arrive at any satisfactory conclusion, there must be common consensus in hermeneutical principles and exegetical practice.

Platform

In any discussion or theological "crossfire," debate rules must be established. Reference points for accurate interpretation must be delineated. One of those reference points for accurate interpretation is the establishment of a final authority.

In theology, there are three possible choices for final authority: Scripture alone, tradition alone, or experience alone. One might be tempted to combine Scripture and tradition, but when these conflict, as for example in the doctrine of the assumption of Mary, a singular final authority must be used. One also might combine Scripture and experience (be it mystical, anecdotal, or rational), but, again, when these conflict, as in miracles or the claim of a special message from God, a singular final authority must be used. The Scriptures must be the final authority, for without this final authority one is open to syncretism, unbiblical mysticism, and doctrinal error.

But even after establishing Scripture as the only final authority, exegetical practice and thought must be regulated by the Scriptural message itself and not be subjected to a utilitarian expectation of what one hopes Scripture supports. The challenge of secularization, Satanic deception, and winsome proposals from the current success-oriented society must all be brought to the foot of Scripture as a final authority. Here is where the Christian worker meets temptation, discerns faith and practice, and must, as well, develop missionary strategy. Accurate biblical exegesis, exposition, and application are his only anchor in interpretation (2 Tim 3:16).

However, it should be observed that there are competing hermeneutical foundations. Among evangelical Protestants there may be difficulty in communication, as illustrated by C. Ray Penn who uses the image of the stresses of hermeneutical tectonic plates clashing beneath the surface. The two plates are *preservationists* and the *expansionists*. The preservationists trace their origin to the Antiochean school of interpretation where the plain meaning of Scripture was sought to express the plain sense of what God intended. The expansionists trace their origin to the Alexandrian School of interpretation where in order to present the gospel to pagans in a winsome way, they allegorized passages which seemed difficult to understand, seemed historically impossible, or seemed inconsistent. The former take a "mathematical" view of hermeneutics whereas the latter prefer an "experiential" perspective (Penn 1989: 341-356). While Penn's original focus was to avoid the pejorative "modernist–fundamentalist" terminology, the same attitude toward hermeneutics is becoming common in today's missiological practice. Penn's observations are directly germane to present hermeneutical practices.

But even with Scripture as the final authority and Antiochean–preservationist hermeneutics, there remains the grave danger of a "canon within a canon." Carson describes this danger as a certain structure or ecclesiastical tradition that adopts a procedure by which it integrates:

> . . . all the books of the canon, and earnestly believe that the structure is not only sanctioned by Scripture, but mandated by it; and as a result, some passages and themes may *automatically* (italics his) be

classified and explained in a particular fashion such that other believers find the tradition in question sub-biblical or too narrow or artificial (Carson 1984:20-24).

This dynamic of a "canon within a canon" may well describe the hermeneutic found in certain proponents of spiritual mapping, identificational repentance, and strategic (cosmos) level spiritual warfare.

This would be, of course, a reductionist error. Intentional or not, a disproportionate amount of attention on certain passages forms a canon within a canon. Carson adds:

Two things will help us to escape from these traps. First, we badly need to listen to one another, especially when we least like what we hear; and second, we need to embark, personally and ecclesiastically, in systematic studies of Scripture that force us to confront the entire spectrum of biblical truth, what Paul calls "the whole counsel of God" (1984:23).

Procedure

With the rich history of evangelical, theological, and missionary preparation, it would seem unnecessary to raise the issue of exegetical procedure. However, the numerous recent publications on hermeneutics show how uncertain some are. David Hesselgrave reminds us that:

. . . one must try to avoid interpretations that may be appealing to the interpreter but are not warranted by the text itself. We Americans are especially vulnerable at this point not only because in our hurried existence we often lack the patience required to learn principles of sound interpretation, but also because Western individualism tends to lead to a respect for every person's opinion no matter how ill-informed it might be (Hesselgrave 1994: 52-53).

Dr. Hesselgrave adds a further exhortation for disciplined Bible study in church and mission ministry:

. . . a much higher priority should be given to instruction in principles of valid interpretation and application of the biblical text in order to avoid unbridled subjectivism (1994:53)

It is not the purpose at hand to develop new criteria for accurate exegesis. The suggestions by Osborne form a solid guide. He suggests eight principles:

1. Consciously reconstruct preunderstanding.

2. Inductively collect all the passages related to the issue.

3. Exegete all passages in their context.

4. Collate all passages into a biblical theology.

5. Trace the developing contextualization of the doctrine through church history.

6. Study competing models of the doctrine.

7. Reformulate or recontextualize the traditional model for the contemporary culture.

8. After individual doctrines are reformulated, begin collating them and reworking the systematic models.

(Osborne 1991: 314-317)

Other writers suggest sound procedures as well. Larkin (1988), Johnson (1990), and Carson (1984) are particularly helpful for the missiologist practitioner. Osborne's final exhortation is noteworthy for us all:

My argument is that this is a threefold process: (1) Inductively, the interpretation appears not from an inspired 0"guess" but from the structural, semantic and syntactical study of the text itself; in other words, it emerges from the text itself, which guides the interpreter to the proper meaning. (2) Deductively, a valid interpretation emerges by testing the results of the inductive research via a comparison with other scholars' theories and historical or background material derived from sources outside the text. One deepens, alters and at times replaces his or her theory on the basis of this external data, which is tested on the basis of coherence, adequacy and comprehensiveness. (3) Sociologically, this proceeds via a "critical realism" that governs an ongoing dialogue between the paradigm or reading communities. The continual challenge and critique from opposing communities drives the individual reader back to a reexamination of the text and his or her reading strategy. As a result the text continues to be the focus and leads one to the true intended meaning (Osborne 1991: 414-415).

Praxis

In the spirit of Carson's encouragement to listen to one another, especially on issues we least like to hear, a case study is in order. There is already much agreement among evangelicals on the need for intercessory prayer for those outside of conscious faith in Christ and the reality of Satanic opposition in world evangelization. Nonetheless, there are differing opinions among equally sincere students about the exegesis and resultant theology of some teaching in the territorial spirits and identificational repentance movement (Brashears 1994: 13-16; Page 1995, Powlison 1995, Van Rheenan 1991, Wakely 1995: 152-162).

The widely distributed work by C. Peter Wagner, *Confronting the Powers*, mailed to all members of the Evangelical Missiological Society, offers a needed case study. Rather than directing attention to multiple authors or even to every debatable point in the case study, a few samples will be taken to serve as examples of weak hermeneutical procedure. Epistemology, while germane, will not be discussed here. Nor will it be to debate the historicity of events not recorded in history books nor remembered in oral tradition. First and foremost is the question, "What does the biblical text teach?"

Evangelicals should concur that:

(1) If anecdotal evidence is contrary to the biblical text, then the anecdote should be rejected.

(2) If the anecdote is neutral or non-supportive of the biblical text, the anecdotal evidence must be held with great caution lest it supplant the primacy of biblical authority. In this instance, the anecdote is, at best, only a possible application.

(3) Of course, if the biblical and anecdotal materials combine in a clear and consistent consensus of interpretation, then the teaching of Scripture is to be embraced, with the anecdote as a supporting illustration.

It is at points two and three that the hermeneutical tectonic plates crash. The criteria for verification submitted by Wagner are sufficient only for an isolated incident. Even he admits being wrong on more than one occasion. In this light, he suggests a checklist to maintain integrity in reporting case studies. However, how one defines a "credible witness" is a great question, not to mention the paramount issue of final authority (1996: 63).

How does this all work out in practice? Attention is now directed to several specifics in a hermeneutical case study:

(1) Identificational Repentance. Central to Wagner's approach to Scripture is identificational repentance whereby corporate confession of national sins by a later generation will lead to the remission of those sins through Jesus' blood and demonic strongholds can be removed. It is viewed that no aspect of prayer warfare is more important than identificational repentance (Wagner, 1996: 260, 30-31, 79, 80, 159, 239). This is also taught by John Dawson (1994: 31), to whom Wagner appeals for support.

A frequent example of this is slavery in America's past, clearly a national evil in history. The issue, however, is applied to breaking Satan's power over cities and individuals due to this past evil. The theological assumption is a covenant relationship whereby the land theme and covenant program of Israel are applied to prayer walks and marches in spiritual battle.

That there is spiritual value in believers uniting in confession and openness, and that spiritual communication be established between ethnic communities is not in doubt. A joint prayer walk can be mightily used in breaking down walls of animosity.

However, the question at hand is the specific use of Old Testament "models" (Dawson: 102) and the covenant structure of Israel in direct relation to issues today. Several issues must be answered satisfactorily before a theological principle can be deducted. First, can any nation today claim those promises that such identificational repentance will lead to spiritual success? Can America claim such a covenant basis as Dawson suggests? While corporate personality has long been established in biblical theology as a strong Old Testament motif, its presence in the New Testament Gentile community of nations in specific use is unclear. Even Wagner admits, " . . . the New Testament contains no outright or explicit teaching about identificational repentance," and that we find relatively little about it in the New Testament (1996: 79).

Notwithstanding, in spite of this confession and repeated circular reasoning by citing Jacobs and Dawson (Wagner 1996: 31, 79, 137, 159, 193, 239), a foundational principle is established as a primary element in this new spiritual technology for completing the great commission.

Additionally, the nature of exegetical procedure itself must be noted. The word "assumption" appears throughout Wagner's works, along with the phrases, "I see," "I think so" (1996: 175-179; 193-194). Not only is biblical exegesis shallow, but the very reasoning process itself begs the question and is circular.

In summary, the recognition of corporate sins among peoples in any country may be a door opener to spiritual awakening. However, weak biblical exegesis linked with anecdotal support, assumptions, and circular reasoning make for a weak hermeneutical foundation to build a doctrine of identificational repentance viewed as central for a strategy of New Testament missiological practice.

(2) Overcoming the Strongman, Binding and Loosing, and Taking the Kingdom by Violence. It is difficult to know where to begin in this mélange of terms used in spiritual warfare literature. In practice, there is a constant interfacing of assumptions and terms without sufficient exegesis. The result is a hermeneutical grid without sufficient substance to construct a doctrine.

Wagner puts great emphasis on *nikao*, "overcoming," and the New Testament imperative for believers to overcome the world. The assumption is that the use in Revelation is the same as that in the gospels, and this becomes a key thesis in spiritual warfare commissioned by Jesus (1996: 144-145). The weakness is not only the indiscriminate linking with a multiplicity of other terms, but that assumptions are made without an inductive study of many other nuances and facets of the terms used (Brown 1975: 650). Wagner fails to comment on the fact that the victory is already won by Christ, expressed in the perfect tense, and that the Lamb's people are secure. Extending the use in Revelation to the use by Jesus in Luke 11:21-22 in order to build a missiological strategy for overcoming the strongman is unsubstantiated.

Furthermore, just who is the "strongman" to be overcome? Wagner is candid when he repeatedly refers to weak support for his position that Beelzebub is not a metaphor for Satan, but a territorial spirit (1996: 146-148). His opinion is that anyone's assumption will form a conclusion based on a previous paradigm. He assumes that Beelzebub is a territorial spirit because the paradigm is based on personal research into the world of darkness. Wagner rejects the opinion that Beelzebub is Satan because the scholars who take this view did not do firsthand research into the world of darkness, but simply rely on other equally inexperienced scholars in the world of darkness. His final conclusion is based on interviews with experts in the occult (1996: 148).

Be that as it may, opinions are bound to differ. The issue, however, is hermeneutical. Wagner clearly states that the conclusion on the identity of the strongman is "crucial to my argument that Jesus commissions us to do strategic level spiritual warfare" (1996: 149). His foundation, however, is assumed (1996: 147) without the benefit to the reader of examining other alternatives.

The next link in the Wagner doctrinal chain is the phrase "binding and loosing" (Matt. 16:19). Without any reference to other opinions, Wagner again assumes a doctrinal framework (1996: 153-156). Basic hermeneutical procedure and exegetical practice are ignored. No other interpretation is considered. The more obvious grammatical and historical approach would point to a rabbinical *asar* and *hitir* halaktic use of the binding and loosing of traditions in the light of Messiah's presence. (Among many exegetes, outstanding are Edersheim 1971: II, 85 and Lachs 1987: 254-257).

Taking the kingdom by violence (Matt. 11:12), by binding the strongman, is another key concept in the chain of phrases (1996: 138). The verb *biazetai* presents well known exegetical difficulties. In spite of this, Wagner simply assumes a conclusion without support. A better model of treating this difficult passage is seen by George Ladd who openly offers six interpretative possibilities and the problems with each when presenting his own conclusion (Ladd, 1974: 158-164).

(3) The use of overly rigid semantics and definitions. Wagner has a strong tendency to make rigid distinctions in sometimes synonymous, or at least interfacing nuances of words. Wagner (1996: 52-55) makes a strong distinction between *rhema* and *logos* even though he states, "although biblical scholars tell us we cannot draw an absolute distinction between the way they are used. . . . a somewhat different meaning *seems* [italics mine] to be attached to each word" (1996: 52). Once again, the argumentation that follows is anecdotal and begs the question. This same weakness is seen in the use of "principalities," "powers," "spirits," and "demons."

Assumptions are seen in other places. Based on shallow evidence, Wagner then uses the word "assumption" four times followed by the phrase, "generally we could say," in proving that a territorial spirit was behind Simon Magus in Acts 8 (1996: 175).

The case of John Mark is treated in the same manner. Wagner's explanation for John Mark's departure is stated as, "my hypothesis is related to this incident of high-level, public power encounter" (1996: 194). His support is a personal incident when he again calls it an hypothesis. Hypothesis notwithstanding, he begs the question. The reader is not helped by careful hermeneutical procedure in a less than clear incident.

One last element is the use of the anecdote itself. For the purposes of this article, one illustration is sufficient. The story of the town of Almolonga in Guatemala and the cult phenomenon of Maximón has interesting facets (1996: 217-220). This writer lived and ministered in Guatemala from 1965 to 1979 at the Central American Theological Seminary and continues to maintain contact in Guatemala. In 1995 he saw personally the cult figure known as Maximón and is intrigued by Wagner's narrative in this regard.

The point is while being careful not to diminish the power of the Holy Spirit over animism in one sector of Guatemala, neither should we diminish His power and work in other areas of Guatemala equally animist. In these other areas the gospel has made significant advances in major towns and people groups without any indication of signs and wonders whatsoever. Rather, the simple preaching of the gospel message (Rom 1:16) has shown its power in transformed lives (Gute 1996).

The point is not the Maximón story itself, but the anecdotal authority that has overtones of prosperity theology and, by journalistic style, implies that such is the case for all of Guatemala. Ultimately, one could not blame a reader who extrapolates a missiological principle for the whole world based on this incident.

Conclusion

In summary, this present article has suggested a simple, but well-recognized procedure for determining the truth of God in these matters. It is no surprise that equally scholarly and godly people will have differing opinions on a particular matter. Of greater significance is their use in the educator-pastoral role of influence beyond what one teaches and publishes. Future Christian workers will be influenced. The lack of sound principles in exegetical practice can lead followers down secondary, if not errant, paths.

It is the conclusion of this article that the strategic level spiritual warfare movement is in danger of departing from Antiochean hermeneutics. This is evidenced by a different attitude toward scriptural authority alone and by a less than objective attitude toward exegetical procedure. The strong tendency is to assume conclusions, thereby making the movement guilty of a canon within a canon hermeneutic.

The final verdict, of course, will come from the Lord of the harvest himself. Time, and ultimately, the larger worldwide body of Christ and the hermeneutical community will have its input. It is imperative that sound hermeneutics be inseparably linked with the filling of the Holy Spirit if we are to understand what the Scriptures teach about the Spirit's role in missionary strategy.

References Cited

Brashears, Gerry
   1994   "The Body of Christ: Prophet, Priest, or King?"
          Journal of the Evangelical Theological Society. Vol. 37
          No. 1.

Brown, Colin. ed.
1975 Article on *Nikao* by W. Gunther in *The New International Dictionary of New Testament Theology*. Vol. I Grand Rapids: Zondervan.

Carson, D. A. ed.
1984 *Biblical Interpretation and the Church*. Grand Rapids: Baker.

Dawson, John
1994 *Healing America's Wounds*. Ventura: Regal Books.

Deere, Jack
1996 *Surprised by the Voice of God*. Grand Rapids: Zondervan.

Edersheim, Alfred
1971 *The Life and Times of Jesus the Messiah*. Parts I and II. Grand Rapids: Eerdmans.

Erickson, Millard J.
1997 *The Evangelical Left*. Grand Rapids: Baker.

Grudem, Wayne A.
1988 *The Gift of Prophecy in the New Testament and Today*. Westchester, IL: Crossway.

Gute, Wayne
1996 "How the Church Grew Among Guatemala's Mam Indians," *Evangelical Missions Quarterly*, Vol. 32 No. 2.

Hesselgrave, David J. ed.
1994 *Scripture and Strategy*. Evangelical Missiological Society Series No. 1. Pasadena: William Carey Library.

Jacobs, Cindy
1993   *Dealing with Strongholds.* Ventura: Regal Books.

Johnson, Elliott E.
1990   *Expository Hermeneutics: An Introduction.* Grand Rapids: Zondervan/Academic.

Kraft, Charles H.
1979   *Christianity In Culture.* Maryknoll, New York: Orbis.

1995   "'Christian Animism'' or God-Given Authority" in *Spiritual Power and Missions.* Evangelical Missiological Society Series No. 3. Pasadena: William Carey Library.

Lachs, Samuel Tobias
1987   *A Rabbinic Commentary on the New Testament.* New York: KTAV Publishing House.

Ladd, George E.
1974   *The Presence of the Future.* Grand Rapids: Eerdmans.

Larkin, William J., Jr.
1988   *Culture and Biblical Hermeneutics: Interpreting and Applying the Authoritative Word in a Relativistic Age.* Grand Rapids: Baker.

McQuilkin, Robertson and Mullen, Bradford
1997   "The Impact of Postmodern Thinking on Evangelical Hermeneutics," *Journal of the Evangelical Theological Society.* Vol. 40, No. 1.

Osborne, Grant R.
1991   *The Hermeneutical Spiral.* Downers Grove: InterVarsity Press.

Page, Sydney H. T.
1995 *Powers of Evil: A Biblical Study of Satan and Demons.*
Grand Rapids: Baker/Apollos.

Penn, C. Ray
1989 "Competing Hermeneutical Foundations and Religious Communication: Why Protestants Can't Understand Each Other." Article taken from *The Journal of Communication and Religion in The Best In Theology,*Vol. III ed. J. I. Packer. Carol Stream, IL: Christianity Today Institute.

Powlison, David
1995 *Power Encounters: Reclaiming Spiritual Warfare.*
Grand Rapids: Baker/Hourglass Books.

Thomas, Robert L.
1996 "Current Hermeneutical Trends: Toward Explanation or Obfuscation?" *Journal of the Evangelical Theological Society.* Vol. 39, No. 2.

Van Rheenen, Gailyn
1991 *Communicating Christ In Animistic Contexts.* Pasadena: William Carey Library.

Wakely, Mike
1995 "A Critical Look at a New 'Key' to Evangelization." *Evangelical Missions Quarterly.* Vol. 31, No. 2.

Wagner, C. Peter
1996 *Confronting the Powers.* Ventura: Regal Books.

10

MODERN AND POSTMODERN SYNCRETISM IN THEOLOGY AND MISSIONS

Gailyn Van Rheenen

A Juncture of Times

Western culture is standing at a juncture of the ages! "The air that we now breathe has changed," says Craig Van Gelder (1996:113). The cultural landscape is changing so rapidly that many mission leaders are struggling to interpret what is occurring. While modern "enlightenment" philosophies focus on the human and disregard the spiritual, postmodern perspectives see humans as molded and shaped by ever-changing human cultures. Walter Brueggemann describes the transition as the creation of a "new interpretive situation" resulting from "a radical shift of categories of culture, for which interpreters of faith in the West have not been well prepared" (1993:1). The postmodernist Walter Truett Anderson is at least partially correct when he says that we are like otters floating on the sea, living in terms of the ebbs and flows of currents without understanding them (1990:ix).

The following two narratives describe the philosophical and cultural changes of the missionary landscape. While reading these narratives, the reader should ask two pertinent questions: To what degree are these missionaries standing above their cultures performing a prophetic function? To what degree are they part of cultural and social forces with which they are only partially cognizant and conversant? Answers to these questions will vary greatly because the reader, rather than being an unbiased spectator, will, of course, interpret these stories from his own experience.

Hopefully, answering these questions will guide the reader's personal journey to rise above the ebb and flow of earthly cultural currents and develop spiritual, God-ordained anchors during the transition from a Modern to a Postmodern Age. The reader will also see how insidious syncretism has impacted Christianity and the Christian mission during both the Modern and Postmodern periods.

Two Narratives: Journeys Missionaries Are Travelling

Recently my wife and I spent the evening with a wonderful missionary family. Over the course of the evening we heard them describe their journey from secular to spiritual living. They testified how God had providentially provided them with a new house, determined when they would return from the mission field to the United States, placed both spouses in their current jobs and ministries, and given spiritual and physical direction to their children. Each story was an experiential vignette describing God's mighty acts in personal life.

I asked them if they had always talked and thought like this. They laughingly acknowledged that they had not. In fact, they lived most of their years as *secular* Christians. Although they believed in God and what He had done through Jesus Christ, they lived and ministered on the basis of their own strength and intellect. On the mission field they learned the language and culture of their recipient people and, by teaching a rational, cognitive message, sought to persuade unbelievers to follow Christ. They nurtured the brokenness of the small Christian community through social therapies learned as part of their Western education. They generally discounted spiritual phenomena as superstition.

They recognize that the movement they helped initiate is static, while the evangelical movement in the same country has experienced phenomenal growth—from three to seventeen percent of the population over the past twenty years. Only in recent years have they come to the conclusion that this lack of growth is because the rational, cognitive orientation of their movement gave little room for God and his Holy Spirit to work.

The husband described returning from the mission field to complete a graduate degree in textual studies at an excellent Christian university. Paradoxically, his cognitively-based education, focusing on historical, grammatical, and critical issues, equipped him to think intellectually yet shook the very foundations of his faith. While becoming proficient in reading the Bible in its original languages, he lost his motivation for Christian ministry. Only in reaction to his education and through influences since returning from the mission field have he and his wife been able to develop a spiritual understanding of life.

The following morning I reflected on the narrative given by C. Peter Wagner at the National Meeting of the Evangelical Missiological Society and noted the similarity to the above story. Wagner has also had a wonderful life of Christian ministry and, during his early years as a missionary and educator, drew heavily upon his modernist heritage. His writings and teaching focused on what would make the church grow. He wrote with confidence that missionaries should develop "church growth eyes," indicating that missionaries should be trained to look at homogeneous groups, expect redemption and lift, and initiate people movements (Wagner 1978). This overriding desire for church growth has been the guiding principle of his life and led him, despite his anti-Pentecostal feelings, to study the rapidly growing Pentecostal Church in Latin America. He wrote,

McGavran taught us that the best way to study church growth was to research the churches which are growing the fastest. In my part of the world, it so happened that the Pentecostal churches were growing much faster than any other kind. So I decided to swallow my pride and see first hand what the Pentecostals in Latin America were doing (Wagner 1996b:4).

During this period, Wagner recounted a "friendly nudge" from Herbert Kane, who wrote: "The proponents of church growth, with few exceptions, have emphasized the human factors and all but overlooked the divine factor." Wagner records that this reflection from an elder statesman of missions startled him and served as his wake-up call (1996b:5).

Wagner's pragmatic search for factors of church growth led him in the 1980s to seek the relationship of signs and wonders to church growth. During these years a primary influence in Wagner's life was John Wimber, church planter of the Anaheim Vineyard Fellowship and author of *Power Evangelism*. In his writings during this period Wagner rightly delineated how God frequently draws people to himself through mighty acts of healing but inadequately depicted how God frequently appears to be quiet, allowing his people to suffer and permitting Satan room to function. Power, illustrated by contemporary and biblical anecdotes, became the focus of his study.

His decision to study the relationship of prayer to church growth, beginning in 1987, led him to develop concepts about spiritual warfare. His basic premise, espoused as Prayer Track coordinator of the A.D. 2000 Movement, was that prayer binds the forces of Satan and enables the mission of God to go forward. Satan is making a stand in his "last fortress," the 10\40 Window. Only the prayers of saints can dislodge him from his position of power.

During this period, Wagner recounted a new *spiritual technology* which would give a major "power boost" to world missions (1996b:7-8; 1996a). The three interrelated elements of this spiritual technology were strategic-level spiritual warfare, spiritual mapping, and identificational repentance. *Strategic-level spiritual warfare* was defined as confrontation with territorial spirits which keep entire geographical regions in spiritual darkness. He equated these territorial spirits with the principalities and powers in Pauline literature and believed that these structures of Satan prevent the spread of the gospel. These powers are discerned by various methodologies of spiritual mapping. This *spiritual mapping* is "research" to detect "where demons are most active and powerful, why they are able to hold on to those powers, and also what their names are" (Wakely 1995:152-53). It is "an attempt to see a city or a nation or the world 'as it really is, not as it appears to be'" (Wagner 1992:151). Spiritual mapping is thought to identify sins of people, cities, or nations frequently committed generations ago, which "have become strongholds of the forces of darkness, allowing them to keep multitudes in physical misery and spiritual captivity" (Wagner 1996:260). *Identificational repentance* is the corporate confession of those sins so that the blood of Jesus covers them and breaks the power of territorial spirits.

It is interesting how Wagner's tone of writing changed over the years. Developing what Wagner termed "church growth eyes" demonstrated his confidence that humans have the ability to know, make decisions, and differentiate. Later writings tell about how God spoke to him and how the Holy Spirit guided him in his work. The following quotes illustrate this change of tone:

We believe we are hearing some of the important things the Spirit is saying to the churches these days, although others may at the same time be hearing equally important, but different words from the Spirit (1996a:14).

At that time I also began hearing the voice of God telling me what my next major assignment would be, namely prayer and how it relates to evangelizing the lost (1996a:16).

As I have said, Lausanne II was the seedbed for the subsequent development of the Spiritual Warfare Network. While in Manila, the Lord spoke to me in a voice that, although not audible, was almost as clear as if it had been: "I want you to take leadership in the area of territorial spirits" (1996a:20).

In various aspects these two life narratives are typical of many who are transitioning from modern to postmodern paradigms. To what degree are they standing above their cultures performing God's prophetic function? To what extent have they been caught up in the cultural currents of their days? First, the cultural currents of the modern period will be described, and then those of the postmodern.

The Modern Era

The transition from the Medieval Period to the Modern era did not occur overnight. Many events served as precursors to the Modern Age. According to Craig Van

Gelder, the *Renaissance*[1] in the 1300s prepared the way for the modern paradigm by refocusing life on the human rather than the spiritual. The *Protestant Reformation* gave impetus to the trend by focusing on the human capacity to "shape their individual and corporate lives." *Expanding economies and the discovery of new worlds* laid the foundations for modern nation-states and colonialism. The concept of natural laws and predictability arose through *new understandings of math and physics*. Astronomers applied these laws to develop understandings of the physical universe. These developments emphasized the role of reason and observation in discovering truth and thus served as precursors to the Enlightenment worldview of the Modern Age (Van Gelder 1996:116).

Various philosophers contributed foundational undergirdings of the Modern Age. *Francis Bacon*[2] (1561-1626) developed the idea that scientific knowledge could be used to master the natural world. Empirical knowledge enabled humans to control the natural world and predict phenomena. Human reason was thought to give power over nature so that it could be used for whatever purpose thought desirable (Hollinger 1994:21-22; Van Gelder 1996:117). As a student, *Rene Descartes* (1596-1650) became disenchanted with medieval religious paradigms. He experienced the traumatic assassination of Henry IV of Navarre, who was about to be crowned King of France and bring anticipated peace and unity to a Europe torn apart by

---

[1]Cultural influences thought to be formative to both Modernity and Postmodernity are italicized throughout this paper.

[2]The names of philosophers whose works are thought to be formative to Modernity and Postmodernity are italicized in this paper.

religious wars. In actions reflecting medieval paradigms, Henry's heart was extracted from his body, displayed throughout France as a religious relic, and finally enshrined at La Fleche, near Paris, where Descartes was a student (Toulmin 1990; Brueggemann 1993:3-4). In reaction to these cultural currents Descartes rejected medieval constructs of reality, based upon the pervasive presence of spiritual powers, and created an alternative paradigm based on the autonomy of the individual self. Security, he felt, could be found only in pure reason, grounded on human objectivity. This Self was able to use reason and observation to determine one's own way in life (Van Gelder 1996:117). The old medieval models were bankrupt, leading to disillusionment. *Thomas Hobbes* (1588-1679) and *John Locke* (1632-1704) applied this rational paradigm to practical models of living within human society. Hobbes emphasized how individuals determine their own self-interest through reason. Locke broadened this agenda to define how the social contract of a culture is determined by rationally defining human rights, obligations, and privileges (Hollinger 1994:22-23; Van Gelder 1996:117). In their own distinctive ways *Adam Smith* related this rational, humanistic worldview to economics, *Emile Durkheim* to sociology, and *Sigmund Freud* to psychoanalysis. Craig Van Gelder adequately defines the modern worldview:

> The autonomous, rational human being was taken to be the starting point for understanding and constructing meaning. Objective science, with its practice of disciplined observation and the logical use of reason, was accepted as the preferred method for developing knowledge, and in this knowledge a dichotomy was established between facts and values. . . . Modernity placed the modern self as an autonomous individual at the center of

life and contended that it functioned by making enlightened rational choices based upon the use of an objective scientific methodology (1996:117, 120).

The world was pictured as "a great machine operating according to unalterable natural laws which could be expressed with great mathematical precision" (Allen 1990:25).

Thomas Oden has proposed a popular dating of the modern era. The era lasted exactly 200 years from the fall of the Bastille in 1789 until the fall of the Berlin Wall in 1989 (1992:32). The Bastille was where the medieval monarchs jailed their political prisoners. Thus when the Bastille was destroyed, "the premodern world with its feudal loyalties and spiritual hierarchies was guillotined" (Veith 1994:27). The French revolutionaries rejected medieval Christianity and enshrined "the Goddess of Reason in the Notre Dame Cathedral" (Veith 1994:27). Thus the French Revolution represented the final end of the medieval period and the triumph of the modern. In a very real sense, the fall of the Berlin Wall symbolizes the fall of secular humanism and the Enlightenment worldview. The Soviet Empire was a government established on the basis of humanistic principles. Christianity was rejected as the "opium of the people." "Marxism, beginning with the assumption of 'dialectical material,' sought to find material, economic causes for all human problems" (Veith 1994:27-28). It was believed that through the rule of the proletariat and the elimination of private property, class struggle and economic exploitation would be eliminated, thereby creating an earthly paradise (Veith 1994:28). When the Berlin Wall fell, its sound echoed around the world. Communist-backed governments in Africa crumbled. An ideological vacuum occurred in many Latin American universities where various forms of Marxism had been espoused. But more profoundly, another nail was pounded into the coffin of modernity.

The Nature of Syncretism

The church has too frequently accommodated to the worldviews of its age. Such accommodation is called *syncretism*. In this context I define syncretism pejoratively to mean *the reshaping of Christian beliefs and practices through cultural accommodation so that they consciously or unconsciously blend with those of the dominant culture*. Or, stated in other words, syncretism is the blending of Christian beliefs and practices with those of the dominant culture so that Christianity speaks with a voice reflective of its culture. Syncretism frequently begins apologetically: The Christian community attempts to make its message and life attractive, alluring, and appealing to those outside the fellowship. Over a period of years the accommodations become routinized, integrated into the narrative story of the Christian community and inseparable from its life. When major worldview changes occur within the dominant culture, the church has difficulty separating the eternals from the temporals. The church tends to loose her moorings because she has for too long been swept along with the ebb and flow of cultural currents. Syncretism thus occurs when Christianity opts into the major cultural assumptions of its society.

The theme of syncretism occurs so frequently in Scripture that it is like a thread interwoven through the fabric of Scripture's kingdom narrative. In a very real sense, the Ten Commandments are injunctions against syncretism. The first three injunctions charge the Israelites to follow Yahweh exclusively—to distinctively stand before God without reliance on any other gods (Exod 20:1-7). The oft-quoted and memorized Shema likewise exhorts Israel to *hear* that Yahweh is one and to love Him with all her heart, soul, and strength (Deut 6:4-5). Moses exhorted the Israelites not to listen to the animistic practitioners prevalent in the land of Canaan but to listen to the prophet like Moses, whom God would raise up (Deut 18:9-15). In other words, Israel was to live distinctively, not fusing the way of God with that of surrounding nations.

Israel, however, did not always listen to Yahweh. God's chosen people incessantly accommodated to the dominant cultures around her and blended their beliefs with hers. For example, Jereboam I, the first king of North Israel, built two golden calves because he feared that his followers might go to the Southern Kingdom and worship Yahweh in the temple. Ahab and Jezebel introduced the Phoenician cult of Baalism into Israel. Manasseh of Judah rebuilt the high places torn down by his father Hezekiah, erected altars of Baal, practiced astrology, and burned his son in the fire as a sacrifice to Molech. Because of this idolatrous syncretism, North Israel was banished into Assyrian captivity (2 Kings 17:16-18) and Judah was exiled for 70 years to Babylon (Jer 11:9-13).

Certain classic statements in the Old Testament describe the nature of syncretism. The Samaritans were a mixed-breed people who also blended their allegiance: "They worshiped the Lord, but they also served their own gods in accordance with the customs of the nations from which they had been brought" (2 Kings 17:33). The pre-exilic Jews partially followed Yahweh but also created for themselves idols out of wood and stone. God, through the prophet Jeremiah, said, "They have turned their backs to me but not their faces, yet when they are in trouble, they say, 'Come and save us!'" (Jer 2:27). Zephaniah spoke of the dual allegiance of the people of Judah, who "bow down and swear by the Lord and who also swear by Molech" (Zeph 1:5).

For the sake of time and space I would like to go from the specific to the general: *There is a tendency for people of God of all times and on all continents to blend their beliefs and practices with that of the dominant culture.* However, as will be seen, the nature and quality of the syncretism varies depending on the dominant culture in which God's community finds itself.

Illustrations of Christianity's Syncretism with Modernity

Ancient Israel frequently syncretized the worship of God with that of the gods. The gods of the Modern Age, however, have not been of wood, stone, or bronze but rational understandings which impede faith and create doubt in the spiritual realm. This focus on humanity and the exclusion of the divine has decimated the church in Western Europe. State churches are empty, and Christianity is disparaged. While the church has greater numbers in North America, she has partially survived by opting into popular culture and seeking to fulfill the felt needs of a consumer-oriented society. The political structures of both the Soviet Union and China, at least until recently, have been overtly secular. Secularization has also spread to the Two-Thirds World through Western-styled schools (who taught laws of nature without connection to the divine) and hospitals (which frequently dispensed medicine for the body without ministering to the spiritual). These schools and hospitals subtly spoke a secular message even when sponsored by the church. The eyes of modernists have been so fixed on the earthlies that they have not been able to see the heavenlies. What are some examples of Christianity's syncretism with modernity?

Christians Becoming "Practicing Deists"

Modernity has led many Christians to become "practicing deists." Charles H. Kraft writes,

> In many ways our Evangelicalism was more like deism than like biblical Christianity. In the New Testament we find Christians appealing to God immediately and insistently whenever a problem occurred. Then, in the guidance, authority, and power received from God they ministered boldly. . . . As Chuck Swindoll has said, "Our God is some distant deity sitting around in heaven answering theological questions." To the extent that such a comment is true, it shows that we have thrown ourselves right into the arms of deism—a Christian heresy spawned by the enlightenment (1989:39).

This deism is reflected by the practices of "enlightenment" Christianity: Christians diligently study the Bible without expecting God to act in the same way as revealed in Scripture. They pray for the sick, yet expect God to work only through doctors' hands. God—who created the world, selected Israel to become his chosen people, and gave resurrection power to his Son—must not be imaged as the classical deist clockmaker. "God wound up the clock of the world once and for all at the beginning, so that it now proceeds as world history without the need for his further involvement" (MacDonald 1984:304-305). Thus to be faithful to the God of the Bible, Christians must break with their Enlightenment heritage to believe that God is "majestic in holiness, awesome in glory, working wonders" (Exod 15:11).

Negation of the Holy Spirit

Similarly "Enlightenment" Christianity does not know what to do with biblical teachings about the Holy Spirit. Some modern Christians have merely equated the Holy Spirit with the Bible, saying that the Holy Spirit operates through the Word and the Word alone. Many have simply disregarded biblical teachings about the Holy Spirit because they are incongruent with modern understandings.

The role of the Holy Spirit is so prevalent in the book of Acts that the book might be called Acts of the Holy Spirit (Van Rheenen 1996:27-28). The topic of the Holy Spirit is introduced in Christ's pre-ascension discussion with his apostles (Acts 1:5-8): the apostles were to receive *power* when the *Holy Spirit* came upon them and, therefore, become Christ's *witnesses* from Jerusalem to the remotest parts of the world. In a real sense these three words—power, the Holy Spirit, and witnesses—describe what God was about to do in the Acts narrative. God's Spirit, not human power, guided the mission!

In the book of Acts the Holy Spirit guided the mission of God in at least three specific ways. First, the Spirit of God guided evangelists to those seeking the way of God. The text specifically said that the "Spirit told Philip" to flag down a chariot (Acts 8:29) and directed Peter to go with the three servants from Cornelius (Acts 10:19). Newbigin, in commenting on Cornelius' conversion, says:

It is certainly true that this story shows how God's mission is not simply an enterprise of the Church. It is a work of the Spirit who goes ahead of the Church, touches the Roman soldier and his household, prepares them for the message, and teaches the Church a new lesson about the scope of God's grace (1989:168).

These passages show God arranging divine encounters so that people seeking him are able to find him. Second, according to the testimony of Acts, the Spirit sets aside leaders for ministry. After fasting, praying, and laying their hands on Barnabas and Saul, the church in Antioch sent them to become the first Gentile missionaries (Acts 13:1-4). This sending was no human endeavor. The Holy Spirit had spoken, "Set aside for me Barnabas and Saul for the work to which I have called them" (Acts 13:2). The church's sending (Acts 13:4) and the Spirit's speaking (Acts 13:3) worked together. The church commissioned and sent out those selected by a praying and fasting fellowship of believers. Third, the Spirit opens and closes doors. In Acts 16 the Spirit closed the doors of Asia (vs 6) and Bithynia (vs 7) but opened the door to Macedonia (vs 9). My family and I experienced God closing the door of Uganda by forcing us to leave during the persecutions of Idi Amin in 1972, but God opened the door to work for thirteen years among the Kipsigis people of Kenya. God has broken the yoke of atheistic Communism, thus opening Eastern Europe and Russia and other previously Marxist countries such as Mozambique, Benin, Angola, and Ethiopia to Christian proclamation.

These examples from Acts challenge the modern tendency to reduce missions to a human endeavor. God, the source of mission, continues to guide his mission through his divine Spirit.

Demythologizing Spiritual Powers

Modernists disavow any powers which cannot be perceived, studied, and analyzed by the five senses. God is relegated to the spiritual realm, where he is allowed little authority over the world he created. Only "natural" powers which can be empirically analyzed are thought to operate in the "natural" world. Paradoxically, people view themselves as self-sufficient, not in need of God in the world that he created. Their world is a "closed universe" because natural powers are thought to operate with no interference from the spiritual realm. Even Christians within secular societies reflect this thinking when they compartmentalize the secular and spiritual. Jeremiah's words call the secular person to dependence on Creator God: "I know, O Lord, that a man's life is not his own; it is not for man to direct his steps" (Jer 10:23).

Western theologians, in particular, have reflected a secular perspective toward spiritual powers. They reflect this secular orientation in three different ways (Van Rheenen 1991:96-98).

The most prevalent response is to simply ignore the powers—to read the Bible without reflecting upon the nature of gods in the Old Testament, demons in the Gospels, and principalities and powers in Pauline literature. Otto Everling's classic quote about the Pauline understanding of angels and demons reflects this modernist stance: "The utterly subordinate significance of this segment of Paul's thought world seems to have become too generally axiomatic for one to give serious attention to it" (1888:4). Walter Wink comments that Western theologians have therefore neglected such studies "precisely because they were *not* easily reducible to modern themes" (1984:102).

A second response is to conclude that, although personal spiritual powers once existed, they no longer exist. The dispensation of their activity came to an end with the death of Christ. Because those holding this perspective see no evidence of present-day activity of spiritual powers, they conclude that the demonic powers were destroyed and no longer exist.

Finally, Western theologians employ various secular paradigms to explain why the powers are not personal spiritual beings. Harnack distinguished between core elements of religion, which are both timeless and eternal, and the temporary garb in which Christianity was clothed in New Testament times. He considered spiritual powers as part of the temporary garb, which was to be discarded (O'Brien 1984). Bultmann perceived personal spiritual powers as representing mythological and, therefore, uncritical thinking. These perspectives had to be "demythologized" and interpreted existentially (MacGregor 1954:26-27). Wesley Carr attempted to prove that all powers in the Bible were angels and that spiritual beings opposed to God did not exist (1987:72). Hendrik Berkhof and Walter Wink sought to prove that spiritual powers do not have a separate spiritual existence but are seen only in the structures of society (Berkhof 1977; Wink 1986). After reviewing these perspectives, one wonders why these Western theologians were forced to find a new paradigm for interpreting spiritual powers in the Bible. Could they not have interpreted the passages literally as personal spiritual beings? Or were their interpretations determined more by a secular mindset than by biblical studies?

Living in the **Present** with Little Regard for the **Past** or the **Future**

The Christian faith is rooted in the understanding that "life is *created* by God and *consummated* by God" (Brueggemann 1993:28). This claim, although crucial to the biblical faith, is out of step with the modern mentality, which believes in neither a creation nor a consummation. "The result of the banishment of an ultimate past and future in the modern world, that is, creation and consummation, is that the present is taken with inordinate and uncritical seriousness, if not absolutized" (Brueggemann 1993:28). The modern man is enculturated to live in the here and now.

Walter Brueggemann calls for the development of an "evangelical infrastructure" which aims to reframe "human reality away from the absolutizing of the present to an appreciation of the past and future" (Brueggemann 1993:28). Mental horizons must be stretched into the past to acknowledge the active hand of God in human history and expanded into the future to acknowledge that "the perishable must clothe itself with the imperishable, the mortal with immortality" (1 Cor 15:53).

The seductive voice of modernity says that we are "finished selves"—that we can live without God. Yet a restless voice within "drives us to despair," revealing wretched slavery to sin and fear of death (Rom 7:23-24). This despair, this hopelessness, is the result of the unrealistic modern expectation that humans can live autonomous lives unrelated to their creator. The counter-cultural voice of the church must, therefore, speak in modern contexts declaring we indeed are "unfinished selves," hopelessly facing death. But God is able through spiritual redemption to bring things to full, glorious completion (Brueggemann 1993:40-41).

Looking back, we are able to perceive the immensity of our cultural accommodation! But is it possible that the current and future cultural accommodations are just as great as those of the past, but merely different? It is to the Postmodern Era that we now turn.

The Postmodern Era

Just as there were many precursors to the Modern Age, so there have been many precursors to the Postmodern Age. The writings of *Immanuel Kant* (1724-1804), especially in *Critique of Pure Reason* (1781), described the nature and limits of human knowledge. He argued that "the external world owes its very shape and structure to the organizing power of the human mind, which imposes order on the chaotic data of the senses" (Veith 1994:36). These ideas gave rise to a steady stream of philosophers and artists throughout the years who, while placing "the autonomous individual at the center of life," emphasized "the subjective, emotional, and creative dimensions of the human condition" (Hollinger 1994:9-11; Van Gelder 1996:119-120).

Early nineteenth-century *Romanticism*, reflecting this Kantian heritage, directly challenged the rationalism of modernity. Romanticists saw nature as a "living organism" rather than as a "vast machine," perceived that God was immanent rather than transcendent, and emphasized emotion over reason as the essence of humanness. Romantic belief in God's immanence sometimes went to the extreme of pantheism: Romanticists denied the separate nature and character of God and described God as a "life force" which animates the entire world, including the individual person. "By getting in touch with one's inner feelings, by intensely experiencing all of life, and by opening oneself up to the splendors of the physical world, a person could `become one with nature' and achieve unity with this life force which animates all of existence" (Veith 1994:35-36). Romanticists idealized living close to nature and criticized the man-made preoccupations of "civilization." They believed that modern technology and materialism corrupt society. "Children are born free, innocent, one with nature." Technologically primitive people were idealized as "noble savages," untainted by the corruptions of development and able to live at one with nature (Veith 1994:36).

Friedrich Nietzsche's nihilism is another forerunner of postmodernism. He declared the death of God and asserted that human beings are unable "to construct any rational meaning for life beyond the will to power" (Van Gelder

1996:120). He described two conflicting attitudes of life, called the Dionysian and the Apollonian. The Dionysian lived instinctually in union with nature, responding to life with vitality; the Apollonian lived under the constraints of imposed "form and order." These resulted in conflicting moralities: the latter "a slave morality, egalitarian, democratic, acquiescing in supposed absolutes" and the former a "master morality that asserts itself with a will to power." Nietzsche believed that only "the will to power . . . can transform human values and create a new *Ubermensch* (superman)" (Holmes 1973:471).

Existentialism also countered the rational forces of modernity and served as a precursor to the Postmodern period. Christian existentialists, like *Soren Kierkegaard* (1813-1855), believed that human experience is foundational to the search for meaning. They believed that "detached, impersonal investigations—as in the natural sciences—cannot deal with the issues such as the meaning of life because they sever the human subject from the object of knowledge. Kierkegaard's aphorism 'Truth is subjectivity' captured the need for human involvement and personal participation in knowledge and truth" (McKim 1991:316). The vast chasm between holy God and sinful man, the incarnation of Christ, and reconciliation of sinful humankind to God through Jesus Christ are absolute paradoxes, based on living faith rather than on human reason. An unbeliever, thus, has to "take a leap of faith" in order to become a follower of Christ (McKim 1991:316-317). Atheistic existentialists, such as *Jean-Paul Sartre* (1905-1980), asserted that since there is no God, "humans must make choices within their historical circumstances and the 'givenness' of their lives. They are responsible only to themselves and encounter the anguish and despair of craving a completeness for life which because of their freedom . . . they can never find" (McKim 1991:317). All values, like other kinds of meaning, are mere human fabrications. Gene Edward Veith describes the relativism of an existential worldview:

> Meaning is not to be discovered in the objective world; rather, meaning is a purely human phenomenon. While there is no readymade meaning in life, individuals can create meaning for themselves. By their own free choices and deliberate actions, human beings can create their own order, a meaning for their life that they and they alone determine. This meaning, however, has no validity for anyone else. No one can provide a meaning for someone else. Everyone must determine his or her own meaning, which must remain private, personal, and unconnected to any sort of objective truth (1994:37-38).

Thus Veith concludes that existentialism furnishes "the rationale for contemporary relativism. . . . [and] is the philosophical basis for postmodernism" (1994:38).

Understandings of the social sciences, reflecting perspectives of *Emile Durkhiem*, greatly impacted how modern people constructed reality. "The autonomous individual who made rational choices out of enlightened self-interest was no longer the key variable in the social equation" (Van Gelder 1996:121). By enculturation the individual grew to become a participating member of society. The socializing impact of the entire culture was thought to be greater than an individual's rational ability to determine his own way. People, therefore, must be studied not merely as individuals but also as participants of cultural movements because every individual was formed by his culture, whether he knew it or not.

While Durkhiem was rethinking the relationship of the person to his culture, Swiss linguist *Ferdinand de Saussure*

(1857-1913) was developing *new perspectives about the nature of language*. De Saussure deduced that meaning is not in the word itself but in the arbitrary meaning assigned to it by members of a culture. A distinction was drawn between the "signifier" (the word) and the "signified" (the meaning). Thus there is no innate relationship between the word "dog" and the pet which my wife and I walk each evening, for this same creature is called "*mbwa*" in Swahili and "*ng'okto*" in the Kenyan vernacular of Kipsigis. There are no "natural connections" between the symbols employed in language and the thing itself (Hollinger 1994:86). Human cultures and cognitive categories within these cultures are thus like languages, "historically constructed within an ever-changing social context" (Van Gelder 1996:122).

This study of the nature of language gave rise to *Structuralism*. The core tenet of Structuralism is that human cultures and cognitive categories within these cultures are like languages, "historically constructed within an ever-changing social context" (Van Gelder 1996:122). Because it effectively dethroned the modern man as the rational master of his universe, this structuralist evaluation was, in a sense, profoundly antihuman. The structuralist, however, perceived the human mind as a unique set of structures demonstrated by its common use of symbols and myth. Steven Best and Douglas Kellner summarize these perspectives:

> The structuralist critique wished to eliminate the concept of the subject which had dominated the philosophical tradition stemming from Descartes through Sartre. The subject was dismissed, or radically decentered, as merely an effect of language, culture, or the unconscious, and denied causal or creative efficacy. Structuralism stressed the derivativeness of subjectivity and meaning in

contrast to the primacy of symbolic systems, the unconscious, and social relations. On this model, meaning was not the creation of the transparent intentions of the autonomous subject; the subject itself was constituted by its relations within language, so that subjectivity was seen as a social and linguistic construct (1991:19).

Structuralists, like Claude Levi-Strauss, thus employed perspectives gleaned from social and linguistic theories to say that human reality is socially constructed. They, however, held these beliefs as social scientists, who believed in "objectivity, coherence, rigor, and truth" (Best and Kellner 1991:20). Thus, although Saussure believed that language is an "arbitrary system," he also "believed that speech gives presence to the world, that the sign has a natural and immediate relation to its referent, and that the signifier stands in a unitary and stable relationship with the signified" (Best and Kellner 1991:20).Structuralists generally held that truth is objective, and reality could be systematically studied although humans were socially formed by influences of language and culture.

Poststructuralism, in turn, viciously attacked the "scientific pretensions" of structuralism. Poststructuralists objected to the structuralist claim of scientific objectivity and said that there are simply no foundations for truth, that truth itself is as much a social construct as language or culture. Thus, according to this perspective, humans are confined to "a prison house of language":

As human beings, we are unable to step outside the boundaries of our language; we cannot escape its limits or its demands. Since language is bound up with our culture, it is largely beyond our control, and we cannot truly think for ourselves. To a large degree, our language thinks for us (Veith 1994:53).

Thus Gene Edward Veith, decrying the postmodern trend, says that Postmodernism is "a worldview that denies all worldviews." The trend is "anti-foundational": "In the past, when one framework for knowledge was thought to be inadequate, it was replaced by another framework. The goal of postmodernism is to do without frameworks for knowledge altogether" (1994:48-49).

The French poststructuralist *Jacques Derrida*, for example, reflecting upon literary theory, developed the concept of *Deconstructionism*. Structuralists were naive, he felt, because they attempted to find the source of meaning within texts; he proposed that the only meaning in a text is what the reader brings to it. "When applied to life, deconstruction demonstrated that everything is to be understood as arbitrary and constructed. It assumes that no inherent value can be found in either the broader social order or the autonomous self of modernity and modernism" (Van Gelder 1996:123). *Jean-Francois Lyotard* stressed the importance of understanding life in terms of narrative. Every narrative, according to Lyotard, has "its own set of rules and self-understanding." He challenged modern thinkers who tried to press all knowledge into prefab models and then insist that experience be interpreted in terms of these paradigms. He focused on different forms of knowledge, believing that "multiple forms cannot be compressed into or subsumed under any kind of grand theory or metanarrative." Life and experience must be interpreted in terms of multiple narratives, each having its own meaning (Van Gelder 1996:128). *Michel Foucault* developed the premise that there is an intrinsic relationship between human knowledge and power. Drawing upon Nietzsche, he "challenged the assumptions that instrumental reason and scientific knowledge are either objective or necessarily rational." He sought to establish that knowledge comes from

188 The Holy Spirit and Mission Dynamics

multiple sources, and Enlightenment thinking, with its emphasis on history and objectivity, obscured "the diverse and plural character of human existence." Social theories, whether economic or social, were considered reductionistic and oppressive. Human knowledge is not to be evaluated by its truth or falsehood but by the power it exerts (Van Gelder 1996:130). *Jean Baudrillard* emphasized that our Western culture is shaped by consumer-driven technology and use of mass media. The mixing of symbols has, over a period of time, blurred the boundary between reality and fiction. Craig Van Gelder summarizes Baudrillard's perspectives:

> Consumer life has become an open marketplace of simulations, of signs, codes, and symbols that blur the distinction between the real and the unreal. We now live in a type of hyperreality in which the model is more real than the real, in which we encounter movies that reconstruct in our consciousness the texts of history, slogans and infomercials that replace political discourse, and technologies of virtual reality that reconstruct a choice of time and place upon demand. This hyperreality has rendered unnecessary the historical connection between a sign and what it signifies (1996:131).

Martin Heidegger attempted to decenter humanity. He attacked the modern perception that humanity is the "center and measure of all things." He constructed a "new humanism," which dethrones humanity as the ruler of the universe and considers him as but one of many creatures. Authentic human experience, according to Heidegger, is not seeking meaning in life but "remaining 'open' to existence, accepting the lack of objective meaning and cultivating a more passive 'openness' to experience as it comes" (Veith 1994:73-74).

Derrida, Lyotard, Foucault, Baudrillard, and Heidegger are all significant philosophers who each have contributed significant components to postmodern thought. However, this description of postmodern thought, because of lack of space and discernment, is by no means complete.

A few broad presuppositions of postmodernity, however, can be ascertained. Generally, postmodernity reflects a radical break with modernity. First, the modern belief that theory reflects reality has disintegrated. It is commonly believed today that one paradigm takes the place of another paradigm which is, in turn, supplanted by still a different paradigm (Kuhn 1970). The postmodern "perspectivist" would conjecture that scientific and philosophical models only partially represent reality. The "relativist" believes that all reality and meaning is historically, socially, and linguistically constructed and there are no ultimate meanings or values. Second, no longer are "macroperspectives on society and history" generally accepted. All broad stokes of understanding are perceived to be simplistic, and microperspectives favored (Best and Kellner 1991:4-5). Third, while the modern mind always sought ways to show that life was orderly, working according to scientific laws of nature, the postmodern mind "accepts, affirms, and embraces the chaos . . . as if that is all there is" (Veith 1994:73). Fourth, modern man sought to study the world while excluding the spiritual. A distinct separation was made between the natural and the supernatural. The postmodern mentality seeks the interrelationship of the natural and the supernatural and is open to various types of spiritual insights.

Illustrations of Christianity's Syncretism
with Postmodernity

Culture's influence upon Christianity is easier to discern in retrospect than in prospect. Christianity's syncretism with modernity is relatively easy to discern because adequate time has passed for reflection and dialogue by various historians and philosophers. Not so with postmodernity. The difficulty in understanding postmodernity is reflected in the name *postmodern* itself. The word literally means "that which replaces modernity." The use of the simple prefix *post-* acknowledges that we do not generally know the directions this new age will take. Perhaps it will be called the *experiential, narrative era*; the *deconstruction epoch*; or the *psychic, supernatural period*. In any case the term *postmodern* will fade away as time allows historians and philosophers to better define the character of the era in which we find ourselves.

If history is our guide, one thing is sure: This age will be as syncretistic as any other. Ancient Israel frequently syncretized the worship of God with that of the gods. Modern "enlightenment" philosophies focused on the human and disregarded the spiritual. What then may be the syncretistic tendencies of the Postmodern Era?

Pervasive Relativism

A most significant area of syncretism during the Postmodern Age involves perceptions about the nature and character of humanity. As we have seen in the first part of this paper, the Modern Age focused on human ability. During this age humans were understood to have rational abilities capable of ordering their own world. Christianity was frequently attacked as illogical and superstitious. Christians themselves were tempted to exclude the divine and emphasize the human. This confidence in human ability tended to enthrone humans as masters of their own world. During the Postmodern Era, however, a philosophical pendulum concerning humanity has swung in a different direction. Human reality is thought to be culturally produced, formed by linguistic and social heritage, rather than by cognitive, rational decisions. Rather than rooted in some eternal truth, reality is thought to be arbitrarily and locally constructed by participants of culture. Life and experience is best interpreted in terms of multiple narratives, each having its own meaning. Cultural meanings are thought to be formed by power struggles within culture rather than by humans seeking truth and searching for meaning. Because of the use of mass media and influence of consumer-driven technology, the postmodern mind frequently is unable to distinguish between truth and fiction. The postmodernist does not necessarily see science and history as truth-based, for these are continually being reinterpreted. Thus the postmodernist lives with a certain ambivalence, acknowledging that objectivity and coherence in life can never be found.

Within this cultural environment the great challenge for Christianity is to *make meaning* where cognitive understanding is considered relative. Allan Bloom says, "There is one thing a professor can be absolutely certain of: almost every student entering the university believes, or says he believes, that truth is relative" (1987:25). Gene Edward Veith concurs:

> The postmodern mind-set can have a devastating impact on the human personality. If there are no absolutes, if truth is relative, then there can be no stability, no meaning in life. If reality is socially constructed, then moral guidelines are only masks

for oppressive power and individual identity is an illusion (1994:72).

Within such relativistic culture Donald C. Posterski encourages us to become *meaning makers*: "Of all the people on the face of the earth, followers of Jesus are in the position to make the most sense out of life because Christians have inside information" (1989:32).

This making of meaning, however, cannot naively circumvent the hermeneutical issues of the Postmodern Age. While maintaining that there is eternal, absolute truth, which has been partially communicated to us through natural and special revelation, Christian meaning makers generally acknowledge that human understandings are perceived through the limitations of language and culture. God, because he is the author of truth and reality, supplies sufficient meaning to respond to him in faith. Ultimately, as Kierkegaard has said, the chasm between humanity and divinity cannot be rationally bridged; it can only be spanned by a living faith. An unbeliever must "take a leap of faith" in order to become a follower of Christ.

Earlier we discussed how pervasive secularism had become during the Modern Age. This faith in human ability eroded the faith of thousands, particularly in Western Europe, and led many other "Christians" to become practicing Deists, especially in North America. One wonders if incipient relativism might be as formidable an opponent of Christian belief during the Postmodern Era. Will God's people be able to maintain Christian meaning in a relativistic age or opt into the dominant ideology of the age—an ideology proclaiming that there is no ideology, that all meaning is relative—thus dethroning humanity as a rational, thinking, decision-making beings?

Finally, an irony. During the age of modernity Christianity was attacked in the name of rationality and humanism Christian theology was ridiculed as superstitious and morality as repressive. The adamant modernist believed that ultimately human reason would displace religious teaching and human values would replace religious values. "Now that the rational and the human are being assaulted, Christians are in the ironic position of having to champion the value of reason and the value of human beings" (Veith 1994:71-72).

Fascination with Spiritual Power

The eclipse of the Modern Age has caused the pendulum to swing from disbelief in the spiritual to fascination with it. Bruce Terry asserts, "The denial of the spiritual by modernity has produced the proliferation of emphases on spiritual powers in postmodernity" (Interview 1997). The key words of our age have become *soul* and *spirit*. Courses entitled Animism or Folk Religion in our Christian schools have low enrollments, but those entitled Spiritual Warfare, Spiritual Formation, or Spiritual Nurture are filled to capacity.

In this cultural milieu New Age perspectives proliferate. Spirituality is interpreted as a peaceful detachment from the world and unity with the cosmos. God is understood to be an impersonal power, like electricity, which permeates all of nature. One New Age adherent, Rosalyn Bruyere, has said, "For me, the terms *God* and *energy* are interchangeable. God is all there is, and energy is all there is, and I can't separate the two" (Reisser 1987:39). Through meditation people are thought to be able to access this "invisible, unmeasured, yet infinite energy which is the basis of all existence" (Reisser 1987:33). Richard J. Foster compares this type of meditation, which has been borrowed from the East, with Christian meditation:

Eastern meditation is an attempt to empty the mind; Christian meditation is an attempt to fill the mind. The two ideas are quite different. Eastern forms of meditation stress the need to become detached from the world. There is an emphasis on losing personhood and individuality and merging with the Cosmic Mind. There is a longing to be freed from the burdens and pains of this life and to be released into the impersonality of Nirvana. Personal identity is lost and, in fact, personality is seen as the ultimate illusion (1988:20-21).

While Christian meditation enables the believer to relate personally with God, New Age meditation leads the adherent to submerge himself in the oneness of the world. Journal articles relating New Age spirituality to feminism, ecology, physical fitness, and therapeutic touch abound.

Many New Age perspectives originate in the East (for example, Reiki healing from Japan and Feng Shui from China) and redefine the world in terms of flows of energy rather than as a personal world "held together" or "sustained" by God through Jesus Christ (Heb 1:3; Col 1:17). Persons playing computer-driven games, like Dungeons and Dragons, Vampires, and Magic, form miniature cultures in which the boundary between reality and fiction frequently blurs as players take upon themselves the attributes of the characters that they play. People seek eternity through reincarnation rather than through a personal, forgiving relationship with creator God. Self-help books emphasize spiritual power to overcome worldly ailments.

This fascination provides many unexpected opportunities to communicate the gospel in terms of spirituality. Recently I travelled from Frankfurt to Prague by train and sat next to a German nurse. She told me of her trips to do "earth" meditation. We had a lengthy discussion about the meaning of earth meditation, how it is done, and the spiritual benefit received from it. She desired to become one with mother earth, to merge her identity with the greater identity of the cosmos, to be lost in the greater whole. After listening and understanding her worldview, I shared with her the meaning of "Christian" meditation. By the end of the journey she understood and appreciated personal meditation based upon relationship with creator God. For the first time I realized that much of Christianity can be understood through the window of meditation. The postmodernist seeking spirituality is likely to be more receptive to the Christian message than the modernist seeking rational understanding of the world.

At least two types of syncretism have emerged during the Postmodern Age.

First, there is a tendency to redefine Christianity in terms of New Age spirituality. A classic example of this trend is a book edited by Duncan S. Ferguson, director of the Committee on Higher Education for the Presbyterian Church (U.S.A.), entitled *New Age Spirituality: An Assessment* (1993). He writes:

> We live in a special time, one of unprecedented change, one filled with overwhelming problems, and one in which people long for a new and nurturing spirituality. It is a critical moment, a *kairos*, and it is out of this moment that the New Age movement has emerged. . . . Our final assumption is that we believe that God is speaking in this movement (1993:x).

A second type of syncretism is an unhealthy and excessive fixation by conservative Christians on the demonic realm. This excessive interest was succinctly expressed by C.S. Lewis in *The Screwtape Letters*:

> There are two equal and opposite errors into which
> our race can fall about devils. One is to disbelieve
> in their existence. The other is to believe, and to feel
> an excessive and unhealthy interest in them. They
> themselves are equally pleased by both errors, and
> hail a materialist and a magician with the same
> delight (1962:3).

C. Peter Wagner's expectation that his new "spiritual technology" will give a "power boost" to world missions is an illustration of such preoccupation. But are Christian servants, with finite understanding and in human form, called to fight territorial spirits? Humans are not involved in cosmic warfare in either Daniel or Revelation, and no leading New Testament commentator has yet to equate the principalities and powers in Ephesians 6:12 to territorial spirits. Are Christians called to map out the demonic hordes in order to plan their defeat based upon the need for "the best possible spiritual intelligence" (1996a:260)? Are not the demons cast out by the power of God rather than by human intelligence? Because Wagner's spiritual mapping entails interviewing demonic spirits, many have called it "missiological syncretism" (Priest, Campbell and Mullens 1995; Powlison 1995; Wakely 1995). Can a "researcher" rely on the realm of deception and lies to provide valid evidence about reality?

This paradigm has more in common with Peretti than Paul. A major theme of Frank Peretti's novel *This Present Darkness* is that the outcome of the battle depends on the believers' use of prayer. Robert A. Guelich, reflecting on this, writes:

> Like air cover for the infantry, one reads repeatedly
> of the insufficiency and the need for adequate
> "prayer cover" for the hosts of heaven before the

engagement can begin. Throughout the story the reader learns that without adequate "prayer cover" the hosts of heaven have no chance against the demonic host. In fact, the marshalling of the "spiritual army" of believers in the town and the recruiting of "warriors" in other cities and countries to provide "prayer cover" for this operation represent the primary war preparations of the "warriors." Indeed, prayer of the Remnant provides the power for the ultimate defeat of the demonic hosts by the hosts of heaven (Guelich 1991:56).

Understandings of territorial spirits and spiritual mapping have roots in Peretti. For example, two of the principal demons in *This Present Darkness*, Ba-al Rahal, Prince of Babylon, and Lucius, Prince of Ashton, are territorial spirits over geographic areas (Guelich 1991:63). In regard to spiritual mapping, determining the number and names of the demons enables the exorcist to cast them out: "Until the Remnant invoked the name of Rafar, this captain of the demonic hosts was gaining the upper hand in his battle with Tal, his arch enemy" (Guelich 1991:56). Guelich's inference is that Wagner's new "spiritual technology" is rooted more in Perettian mythology than in the biblical text. As in much postmodern rhetoric, the line between reality and fiction is blurred so that Peretti's fiction is interpreted as reality.

The dangers of this focus on the demonic are numerous. Too frequently missionaries focus on the dominion of Satan rather than the kingdom of God. They become frightened by the presence of animistic idols rather than realizing that an idol is nothing before the Creator. Rather than walking triumphantly in the heavenlies far above the principalities and powers, they walk in the earthlies fearful of the demonic horde.

Focusing on Power and Neglecting Truth

A third area of syncretism during the Postmodern Age is focusing on power and neglecting truth. God, to be sure, is all powerful. He is "majestic in holiness, awesome in glory, working wonders" (Exod 15:11). Not only is God's power quantitatively greater than Satan's; its *quality* is also different. Satan's power is debasing—contorting the disobedient who follow the cravings of their own sinful nature (Eph 2:3). God's power, based on his great love, raises us above these earthly cravings into heavenly realms (Eph 2:4-6). Paul's prayer of Ephesians 3:14-21 interweaves God's power with his great love.

When Christianity is reduced to power, the Christian message is always significantly distorted. God's power must always be seen in a broader theological framework. For example, sometimes sovereign God, who has all ultimate power, decides not to act. Perhaps he is allowing Satan to test his people; perhaps he desires that his people learn obedience in suffering. At such times the people of God lament, crying, "We have heard with our ears, . . . our fathers have told us what you did in their days" (Ps 44:1), but "Why do you hide your face?" (Ps 44:24). Although the modern negation of divine power must be challenged, the concept of power must be placed in an eschatological framework: Sometimes the God of all power decides not to act, although at the end of time all powers will be made obedient to him.

Our previous description indicates why postmodern culture has shifted from "truth" to "power." Postmodern perception that truth claims are only social constructs and, therefore, not inherently true has led many to believe that these understandings are based merely on power. According to the postmodern, even church leaders base their decisions on power rather than truth. Because of the increasing acceptance that power is the issue of the age, the church, in an attempt to be relevant, has begun to focus on power. This tendency to focus on power and shift away from proclamation of truth is addressed by the Lausanne Committee on Spiritual Warfare:

> The tendency to shift the emphasis to "power" and away from "truth" forgets that error, ignorance and deception can only be countered by Biblical truth clearly and consistently taught. This is equally, if not more important than tackling bondage and possession by "power encounters." It is also the truth that sets us free, so the Word and the Spirit need to be kept in balance. (1993:3).

Neil T. Anderson's booklet *Winning Spiritual Warfare: Steps to Freedom in Christ* (an excerpt from *The Bondage Breaker*) gives a balance between truth and power:

> I don't believe in instant maturity, but I do believe in instant freedom, and I have seen thousands of people set free by the truth. Once a person is free, you would be amazed at how quickly he or she matures! (1990:8)

This statement from The Willowbank Report is an important reminder for Christians living in the Postmodern Age with its emphasis on power: "Power in human hands is always dangerous. We have to mind the recurring theme of Paul's two letters to the Corinthians—that God's power, which is clearly seen in the cross of Christ, operates through human weakness (e.g., 1 Cor 1:18-2:5; 2 Cor 4:7; 12:9-10).

Worldly people worship power; Christians who have it know its perils" (Stott and Coote 1980:327).

Interpreting Emotions and Intuition as the Work of the Holy Spirit

During the Postmodern Age, Christians are building new mental frameworks about the Holy Spirit based on popular parlance. Increasingly, they interpret their emotions and intuition as the working of the Holy Spirit. This perception is reflected in the oft-heard statement: "Be quiet and listen to God." The starting point is experience rather than natural or special revelation. For example, Peter Wagner's earlier quotes describe all of his plans as originating from the Holy Spirit or God:

> "We are hearing some of the important things the Spirit is saying to the churches . . . others may at the same time be hearing equally important, but different words from the Spirit" (1996a:14). "I also began hearing the voice of God telling me what my next major assignment would be, namely, prayer and how it relates to evangelizing the lost" (1996a:16). "The Lord spoke to me in voice that, although not audible, was almost as clear as if it had been: "I want you to take leadership in the area of territorial spirits" (1996a:20).

The biblical heritage of God speaking through the prophets to the community is reinterpreted during the Postmodern Age as God speaking to each individual person for [because] all are understood to be God's prophets. Bruce Terry expresses this in postmodern jargon: "The Postmodernist says, 'When I have a intuition it is the Holy Spirit speaking to me. When I have an emotion, it has been generated by the Holy Spirit'" (Terry 1997). Thus Christians build a schema about the Holy Spirit, but the model starts with experience and is rooted in intuition. Biblical language is used, but it is formed out of popular narratives.

Final Reflections on the Narratives

In writing this paper I have become aware of how much the influences of the Modern and Postmodern Ages have shaped my life. I was born into a modern world and will die in a postmodern one. While I was missionary on the field, the questions I asked were all basic questions concerning my enculturation within modern social constructs while working in a non-Western context: Are there spiritual powers? Who is God? What is the relationship between God and the gods? If God is active, what is the role of science and scientific inquiry? Does God work on the basis of laws of nature, or does the orderliness of the world reflect the nature of the God who sustains it? Have we placed too much confidence in human abilities and human ingenuity? (Van Rheenen 1996:129-130). Only now, after writing this paper, have I begun to struggle with my own postmodern syncretisms. Amazingly, I have found many of my tendencies are very similar to those of C. Peter Wagner and the couple that I have used as the first illustration. I thank these people for their narratives; I have personally grown by interacting with them. These people and their stories have become my teachers, not only about missions but also about the Modern and Postmodern cultural currents influencing the church and its missions to the world.

References

Allen, Diogenes
1989 *Christian Belief in a Postmodern World: The Full Wealth of Conviction.* Louisville, KY: Westminster /John Knox Press.

Allen, C. Leonard
1990 *The Cruciform Church: Becoming a Cross-Shaped People in a Secular World.* Abilene, TX: Abilene Christian University Press.

Anderson, Neil T.
1990 *Winning Spiritual Warfare: Steps to Freedom in Christ.* Eugene, OR: Harvest House.

Anderson, Walter Truett
1990 *Reality Isn't What It Used to Be.* New York: Harper and Row.

Berkof, Hendrik
1977 *Christ and the Powers.* Rev. ed. Translated by John H. Yoder. Scottdale, PA: Herald.

Best, Steven and Douglas Kellner
1991 *Postmodern Theory: Critical Interrogations.* New York: The Guilford Press.

Bloom, Allan
1987 *The Closing of the American Mind.* New York: Simon and Schuster.

Brueggemann, Walter
1993 *Notes under Negotiation: The Bible and Postmodern Imagination.* Minneapolis: Fortress Press.

Carr, Wesley
1987 *Angels and Principalities.* Cambridge: Cambridge University Press.

Everling, Otto
1888 *Die paulinische Angelologie und Damonologie.* Quoted in Hendrik Berkhof. *Christ and the Powers.* 1977. Scottdale, PA: Herald.

Ferguson, Duncan S., ed.
1993 *New Age Spirituality: An Assessment.* Louisville: John Knox Press.

Foster, Richard J.
1988 *Celebration of Discipline.* San Francisco: Harper.

Guelich, Robert A.
1991 Spiritual Warfare: Jesus, Paul and Peretti. *PNEUMA: The Journal of the Society for Pentecostal Studies* 13 (Spring): 33-64.

Hollinger, Robert
1994 *Postmodernism and the Social Sciences: A Thematic Approach.* Thousand Oaks, CA: Sage Publications.

Kraft, Charles H.
1989 *Christianity with Power.* Ann Arbor MI: Vine Books.

Lamar, James S.
1859 *The Organon of Scripture: Or, the Inductive Method of Biblical Interpretation.* Philadelphia.

Lausanne Committee for World Evangelization
1993 Statement on spiritual warfare. Press Release, August 27.

Lewis, C.S.
1962   *The Screwtape Letters.* New York: Macmillan.

MacDonald, Michael
1984   Deism. In *Evangelical Dictionary of Theology*, ed. Walter A. Elwell. Grand Rapids: Baker.

MacGregor, G.H.C.
1954   Principalities and Powers: The Cosmic Background of Paul's Thought. *New Testament Studies* 1 (January): 17-28.

McKim, Donald
1991   Christian Existentialism. In *Encyclopedia of Religious Knowledge*, ed. J.D. Douglas, 2d. ed., 316-17. Grand Rapids: Baker.

Newbigin, Lesslie
1989   *Gospel in a Pluralist Society.* Grand Rapids: Eerdmans.

O'Brien, P.T.
1984   Principalities and Powers: Opponents of the Church. In *Biblical Interpretation and the Church*, ed. D. A. Carson, 110-50. Nashville: Thomas Nelson.

Oden, Thomas C.
1990   *After Modernity . . . What?: Agenda for Theology.* Grand Rapids: Academie Books.

1992   *Two Worlds: Notes on the Death of Modernity in America and Russia.* Downers Grove, IL: InterVarsity.

Peretti, Frank E.
1986 *This Present Darkness.* Westchester, IL: Crossway.

Powlison, David.
1995 *Power Encounters: Reclaiming Spiritual Warfare.* Grand Rapids: Baker.

Posterski, Donald C.
1989 *Reinventing Evangelism: New Strategies for Presenting Christ in Today's World.* Downer Grove, IL: InterVarsity.

Priest,Robert J., Thomas Campbell, and Bradford A. Mullen
1995 Missiological Sycretism: The New Animistic Paradigm. In *Spiritual Power and Missions: Raising the Issues*, ed. Edward Rommen, 9-87. Pasadena, CA: William Carey Library, 1995.

Reisser, Paul C., Teri K. Reisser, and John Weldon
1987 *New Age Medicine.* Downers Grove, IL: InterVarsity.

Stewart, James
1951 On a Neglected Emphasis in New Testament Theology. *Scottish Journal of Theology* 4:291-301.

Stott, John R.W. and Robert Coote, eds.
1980 *Down to Earth: Studies in Christianity and Culture.* Grand Rapids: Eerdmans.

Terry, Bruce
1997 Personal Interview. June 8 in Abilene, TX.

Toulmin, Stephen

1990　*Cosmopolis: The Hidden Agenda of Modernity.* New York: Free Press.

Van Gelder, Craig
1996　A Great New Fact of Our Day: America as Mission Field. In *The Church between Gospel and Culture,* ed. George R. Hunsberger and Craig Van Gelder, 57-68. Grand Rapids: Eerdmans.

1996　Mission in the Emerging Postmodern Condition. In *The Church between Gospel and Culture,* ed. George R. Hunsberger and Craig Van Gelder, 113-138. Grand Rapids: Eerdmans.

Van Rheenen, Gailyn
1991　*Communicating Christ in Animistic Contexts,* 2d ed. Pasadena: Wm. Carey Library.

Van Rheenen, Gailyn
1996　*Missions: Biblical Foundations and Contemporary Strategies.* Grand Rapids: Zondervan.

Veith, Gene Edward Jr.
1994　*Postmodern Times: A Christian Guide to Contemporary Thought and Culture.* Wheaton: Crossway Books.

Wagner, C. Peter
1978　*Church Growth Principles and Procedures.* Syllabus and Lecture Outlines. Pasadena: Fuller Theological Seminary.

1992　*Warfare Prayer.* Ventura, CA: Regal Books.

1996a *Confronting the Powers: How the New Testament Church Experienced the Power of Strategic-Level Spiritual Warfare.* Ventura, CA: Regal Books.

1996b *Contemporary Dynamics of the Holy Spirit in Missions: A Personal Pilgrimage.* Speech made at the National Meeting of the Evangelical Missiological Society. Sept. 22.

Wakely, Mike
1995   A Critical Look at a New 'Key' to Evangelization. *Evangelical Missions Quarterly* 2 (April 1995):152-62.

Wink, Walter
1984   *Naming the Powers: The Language of Power in the New Testament.* Philadelphia: Fortress.

1986   *Unmasking the Powers: The Invisible Forces That Determine Human Existence.* Philadelphia: Fortress.

OTHER MISSION BOOKS FROM
WILLIAM CAREY LIBRARY
For a complete catalog write:
William Carey Library
P. O. Box 40129
Pasadena, CA 91114

CHRISTIANITY AND THE RELIGIONS: A Biblical Theology of World Religions, EMS #2, Ed Rommen, editor, 1995, 300 pages.
The current discussion on the Christian attitude towards non-Christian religions is one of the most critical theological debates of our day, This study focuses on the Christian view of non-Christian religions and takes as a given the uniqueness of Christ.

COMMUNICATING CHRIST IN ANIMISTIC CONTEXTS, by Gailyn Van Rheenen, 1996, paperback, 344 pages.
Communicating Christ in Animistic Contexts shows that animistic beliefs are ubiquitous today, whether in New Age mysticism, horoscope occultism, Haitian voodooism, Chinese ancestor veneration, or Japanese Shintoism. Gailyn Van Rheenen presents a rigorous biblical, theological, and anthropological foundation for ministering in animistic contexts overseas or next door.

CUSTOMS AND CULTURES: Anthropology for Christian Missions (Revised), by Eugene Nida, 1997, 350 pages.
In this carefully revised edition the dean of Christian anthropologists continues to meet the need of an anthropology for Christian missions as each chapter shows wide kn owledge of racial, tribal and human customs.

CRISIS AND HOPE IN LATIN AMERICA: An Evangelical Perspective (Revised Edition), by Emilio Antonio Nunez C. and William David Taylor, 1996, paperback, 544 pages.
Nunez and Taylor expand their earlier work on Latin America. This revision incorporates an insightful essay by Peruvian missiologist Samuel Escobar, an updated section by Nunez and Taylor, and an expanded annotated bibliography.

DAWN 2000: Seven Million Churches to Go. The Personal Story of the DAWN Strategy by James Montgomery 1989, paperback, 24 pages.
Of all the strategies to evangelize the world, the concept of national-level collaboration is probably the most crucial and essential. This

book by a competent writer is a beautiful, personal unfolding of what is now a movement at work in twenty-six nations. You will not be able to put it down!

MEDIA IN CHURCH AND MISSION: Communicating the Gospel, by Viggo Sogaard, 1993, paperback, 304 pages.
A readable and practical synthesis of what has been learned through the new wave of thinking about communications.

MISSIOLOGY AND THE SOCIAL SCIENCES, EMS#4, Edward Rommen and Gary Corwin, editors, 1996, paperback, 232 pages.
This book is the fourth in the Evangelical Missiological Society Series. The contributors look at the relationship between the social sciences and missiology and seek to explain the scope and limitations of their discipline in forming the science of missiology.

MESSAGE AND MISSION: The Communication of the Christian Faith (Revised), by Eugene A. Nida, 1990, paperback, 300 pages.
Sharing the Christian life and truth is far more than using words and forms congenial to us, but strange and perhaps threatening in another culture. This book not only points the way to true communication but is foundational in this field.

PERSPECTIVES ON THE WORLD CHRISTIAN MOVEMENT: A Reader (Revised Edition), Ralph D. Winter and Steven C. Hawthorne, editors, 1992, paperback, 944 pages.
This text was designed to be the missionary platform of essential knowledge for all serious Christians who have only a secular education. Used as a basis for mission courses for fifteen years.

A PEOPLE FOR HIS NAME: A Church-Based Missions Strategy by Paul A. Beals, 1994, paperback, 260 pages.
A masterful overview of the roles of local churches, mission boards, missionaries and theological schools in the biblical fulfillment of the Great Commission.

PREPARING MISSIONARIES FOR INTERCULTURAL COMMUNICATION: A Bicultural Approach, by Lyman E. Reed, 1985, 216 pages.
Missionaries,while being prepared in the Bible, often receive little training in understanding the world in which we live and frequently experience difficulties on the field as a result. How to be prepared for cross-cultural ministry is the focus of this volume.

RESEARCH IN CHURCH AND MISSIONS, by Viggo Søgaard, 1996, paperback, 280 pages.

A very useful instructional base for both the student learning the fundamentals of communication research and for the administrator of a research project. A base of communication theory sets the stage for the research methods in this book. Søgaard's worldwide consulting experience in communication research puts under one cover why and how systematic research methods and skills should be and could be used to improve effectiveness of Christian ministries.

SCRIPTURE AND STRATEGY: The Use of the Bible in Postmodern Church and Mission, EMS#1, by David J. Hesselgrave, 1994, 192 pages.

The first volume in the Evangelical Missiological Society Series, David Hesselgrave uses the work of ten influential men to describe what is going on in missions. Each chapter deals with a different aspect of the use of the Bible in the church and mission.

ST. LUKE'S MISSIOLOGY: A Cross-Cultural Challenge, by Harold Dollar, 1996, paperback, 198 pages.

An exemplary integrative study with missiological conclusions that are weighty because they are firmly anchored in careful, multidimensional biblical scholarship.

TRANSCULTURATION: The Cultural Factor in Translation and Other Communication Tasks, by R. Daniel Shaw, 1988, 300 pages.

Transculturation accomplishes for the cultural and non-verbal aspects of communication what translation has done with verbal and literary forms. On this premise Dr. Shaw demonstrates that transculturation is a process of information transfer that takes the whole translation context into account and allows people to respond in a way that is natural and appropriate for them.